Emmeline and Her Daughters

THE PANKHURST SUFFRAGETTES

IRIS NOBLE

BAILEY BROTHERS AND SWINFEN LTD.
Folkestone

Published in Great Britain by
Bailey Brothers and Swinfen Ltd.
1974
Copyright © 1971 by Iris Noble. All Rights Reserved
SBN 561 00222 3

Printed in Great Britain by
Whitstable Litho, Straker Brothers Ltd.

~//~ Chapter one

Emmeline Pankhurst straightened the cushions on the sofa, brushed cake crumbs from a small table and handed the tea tray to the maid. She glanced at her husband, who was sitting by the fire and staring into it, moved suddenly as if to go to him and then checked herself. She would not disturb him just yet.

Tall and slender as she was, every motion she made was graceful as she tidied up the room, but today there was an added restlessness of anger in her movements that made her long skirts flick and swirl along the carpet. A hairpin had come loose in the jet-black curls piled high on her head. She jabbed it back with a furious gesture.

It was outrageous, she thought, that her husband should be made to look so sad, so worn and despairing. Everyone knew how splendid and brilliant he was, yet again that afternoon he had met with nothing but disappointment.

A suffrage group had met as usual that Saturday of 1892 at the Pankhurst home in London, and as usual Dr. Pankhurst had spoken eloquently on the subject of women's right to the vote. Everyone had applauded him, but—as always—no one had anything hopeful to say when he finished.

He had expected something better from Keir Hardie, who had just been elected to the House of Commons, but Hardie had made a discouraging report. He was too new in the House to have any influence yet. As a former coal miner he dressed and spoke like a workman, and the other members of Parliament shunned him. When he tried to talk of the rights of women, they laughed at him.

Women had no rights, they said, and that was how God intended it to be. Females with brains were unnatural creatures. It was the duty of men to protect, govern and guide the weaker sex and the duty of women to obey without question. It was unthinkable that they should vote or hold national office. The nation would be ruined.

At that time in Britain women could not vote, hold office or enter any profession except teaching or nursing. If a woman inherited property, her husband controlled it when she married; if she left her husband, he kept her fortune; it was his legal right to make all decisions regarding her or their children.

Emmeline picked up a small embroidered bag which held the collection taken up at the meeting and emptied its contents on to the table. So few coins! Tears of frustration came to her eyes, but she winked them back as she saw her three daughters enter the room, their dresses changed and their hands washed in readiness for supper.

"You behaved very nicely today at the meeting," she

told them. "I was proud of you. Mr. Hardie said you listened more closely to him than members of the House do."

Sylvia, aged ten, said, shyly, "I liked him. He was kind."

But twelve-year-old Christabel, as pretty as a porcelain figure, with her dark hair and pink-and-white complexion, wrinkled her small, perfect nose and said: "Why does he wear that cloth cap and that red kerchief? He's not a gentleman, is he?"

Little Adela, only seven, said nothing but took herself and her doll over to the fireplace to lean against her father's knee. He moved a hand to touch her hair, and Emmeline thought it was time to rouse him from his despondency. She went to his side, smiled down at him and reached out to touch him.

To her great astonishment he pushed her arm away. So vehement was his gesture that even little Adela fell forward on to the cushioned ottoman at his feet. He glared up at his wife, almost as if he didn't recognize her, and burst out:

"Why don't you *force* us to give you the vote? Why don't you scratch our eyes out!"

For a moment Emmeline could only stare at him with the same consternation in her eyes as was in her daughters'. Never had she heard her dignified husband speak so violently. Dr. Pankhurst was a reserved man, full of responsibilities but always gentle and tender towards his family. Even little Adela hushed her whimper as she gazed, shocked, at her father.

Then Emmeline felt in herself a surge of an emotion

long repressed. Oh, he was right! How often had she longed to scratch out the eyes of all the nameless men who looked upon her as an inferior being just because she was a woman.

"But," she said, "how can we *force* men to give us the vote when we are so powerless? I think almost all women in Britain must resent the way they are treated, but so few of them ever dare to speak up for their rights."

Dr. Pankhurst's face relaxed, and he smiled at her and pulled Adela on to his lap. He held out his other arm to embrace Sylvia. "I know, my dear. I know. It is not to be expected that our women, held so long in bondage, should know how to lead a crusade for themselves. Yet someday I think they must." He relaxed back in his chair. Adela began telling him a complex story about an imaginary cat.

But Emmeline was still in the grip of an excitement new to her. She was thrilling to a most astounding idea. Was it possible she could lead instead of following? What would it be like to be the one to lead a crusade? To demand, instead of beg! To *force* men to give women their rights! The thought was intoxicating.

Her eyes met Christabel's, and she saw her own excitement reflected in the girl's. Sylvia and Adela were happily snuggled against their father's shoulders, but Christabel's attention was on her mother and, as happened so often, they understood each other without speaking. Emmeline, with her sea-blue eyes and the finely shaped bones of her face, and Christabel, in her dainty prettiness, were the most "feminine" ones of the family, but they were also the ones with the strongest wills and clearest purposes.

Christabel's hands were clenched; when Emmeline saw that, she smiled. Yes, this girl had it in her to fight and the wish to "scratch their eyes out."

The strange moment of excitement passed. Emmeline came back to reality. Who was she—a gentlewoman, the mother of four children and the wife of an eminent man —to think of pounding her umbrella over the heads of arrogant males or raising her hand to them? The idea was best forgotten.

The maid led in three-year-old Harry, toddling on plump legs, and Emmeline took him on to her lap, sitting across the fire from her husband. She heard him explain to his daughters how fine a man Mr. Hardie was and how much he was doing to help the poor and unemployed of Britain.

But that made Emmeline think of their own poverty. She greatly loved this crusader husband of hers, but she could wish he were more practical. He was a doctor of laws of London University and a member of the National Association for the Promotion of Social Science, the Royal Statistical Society and many other organizations; he was a learned and brilliant man, but he rarely knew where his next penny was coming from.

He was constantly losing clients because of his outspoken ideas. He was a founder of the new Liberal Party. The other Liberal leaders sought him to draw up the acts and bills they would present in Parliament; but when he stood for election to the House of Commons, they would not support him and he was defeated.

He was too radical, they said. They could forgive his calling himself a "socialist" but not for advocating votes for women. That was going too far.

Emmeline was bitter about it, far more than he was. After all, it was she who had to make the petty economies, sew their clothes, buy the cheaper cuts of meat and darn the tears in sheets and upholstery. She had even opened a fancy-goods shop in London, but she was not gifted with business sense and it was a failure.

She was not used to penny-pinching. Born Emmeline Goulden in 1858, thirty-four years before, she had been the oldest and favourite child of Robert Goulden, a well-to-do Manchester businessman. She had been brought up in comfort, had attended a fashionable "dames" school and had even spent two years in a Paris finishing school.

Not that she regretted marrying Dr. Pankhurst or any of the sacrifices she made for him. He was twenty years older than she, but a hero in her eyes. What other man would have treated her as his equal, encouraged her to think and use her intelligence?

No one else. Her father had professed to be a liberal thinker, and she knew he loved her, but as he said, "it was a pity she was a girl." And as a girl she was not entitled to a good education. His five sons were well schooled to fit them for professions, but his five daughters were destined only for marriage, and learning to read and write, doing embroidery and playing the piano were enough for them. The French finishing school for Emmeline was a great indulgence on the part of her father, but even there she learned only to speak French fluently and develop an elegant style in her gowns.

No, Emmeline had known what she was doing when she braved her father's wrath to marry Dr. Pankhurst. Robert Goulden had much admiration for the Doctor, but he was not the husband chosen for his daughter's hand. He would never make any money, and he was putting outrageous ideas in Emmeline's head. Dr. Pankhurst even declared that Emmeline must try to speak at public meetings. Robert Goulden answered that the shame of such a thing would bring him to his grave.

Emmeline, rocking her son in her arms, smiled to herself. In spite of her eager response to her husband's teachings, she trembled at the knees if she had only to get up in a meeting and say, "I second the motion." She doubted she would ever be a public figure.

Her husband thought otherwise.

In the next years that passed, he often reminded Emmeline of his outburst that night, and he felt there was truth in it. If women were to achieve their rights, he said, they could not depend upon a handful of men to do it for them. Women must unite and must strongly press their demands, and any effective organization must have women leaders who were strong and forceful and confident.

He spent more and more time educating her. He was not very successful in getting her to read heavy books on economics or philosophy or law; she much preferred light novels. But she was quick to learn about people from observation, and so he took her with him whenever he went to meetings or to the House of Commons. She heard the debates from the Ladies' Gallery, and in the

anterooms of the House chamber Dr. Pankhurst introduced her to the leading Parliamentarians.

Emmeline was aware that they admired her for her
beauty, not her brains. She had enough vanity to be
pleased at their admiration. Her figure was slim and her
carriage erect, and she knew her eyes would seem blue
when shaded by a large plumed hat or greenish when she
put a lemon-yellow flower under the brim of a poke
bonnet. But she listened more closely to the political con-
versations than the gallant gentlemen expected of a
pretty woman.

The family had to move back to Manchester, where
Dr. Pankhurst's legal office was. Even then their lives
were full of political meetings and conferences.

In July of 1889, before the Pankhursts left London, a
group had gathered at their home to form the Women's
Franchise League. The founders of the league were the
Pankhursts; Mr. and Mrs. Jacob Bright, of Manchester;
the elderly Elizabeth Wolstenholme Elmy and her hus-
band, Ben; Josephine Butler; Cunningham Graham;
Jane Cobden; Lady Sandhurst; and Mrs. P. A. Taylor.
Also present at that meeting were special guests from
America; Elizabeth Cady Stanton and William Lloyd
Garrison, both pioneers in the struggle for woman suf-
frage and for abolition of slavery.

There were other woman suffrage organizations, but
Dr. Pankhurst considered them little more than polite
educational societies. The new league would be free to
work within the Liberal and Labour parties.

However, when the Pankhursts came back to Manchester, they found that the Liberal Party's burning issue

was not votes for women but unemployment. Great numbers of men and women were out of work and hungry.
Dr. Pankhurst and Emmeline threw themselves into the
task of helping to feed those who could not afford bread
and leading the unemployed in protest marches and
demonstrations.

Robert Goulden did not like it at all when he saw his
daughter, Emmeline, standing up in a cart on a public
street dispensing soup and bread to a line of poorly clad
men.

But, worse still, she made her first public speech at an
open-air demonstration to demand that civic leaders give
jobs to men out of work. Her knees had trembled and
her voice shook, but her courage carried her through it
and she was rightfully proud of herself. Mr. Goulden was
scandalized. If Emmeline was going to indulge in such
unwomanly behaviour, she was no longer welcome in his
house, and from that time on there was a split between
herself and her parents that never healed. She remained
friends with several of her brothers and sisters, but only
one—Mary—really approved of her work.

Once Emmeline had recovered from her fear of public
speaking, she was intoxicated by it. She found, to her
amazement, that she had only to walk on to a platform to
command people's immediate attention, that she always
seemed to find the right and simple things to say and that
she was born with a dramatic flair.

Dr. Pankhurst was more learned, but not nearly so
effective a speaker. Besides, though he kept it a secret
from his wife, his health was beginning to fail. He
pushed her forward instead of himself.

In 1894 there was a small triumph for woman suffrage. Parliament passed the Local Governments Act, giving more power to local city, town or borough governments and including the astounding clause that women could be elected to such bodies. The Liberal Party immediately acknowledged the rising prominence of Emmeline Pankhurst by choosing her as their candidate for the July, 1894, Manchester School Board election.

She lost that election, but shortly afterwards she won another and was elected by the Chorlton district of Manchester to their Board of Guardians.

The work of the Guardians was to look after the poor of the district, which to the male members of the board meant only the management of the poorhouse, the workhouse and the home for the aged and the orphans. Emmeline had other ideas. In this time of frightful unemployment she felt they should concern themselves also with those out of work. So Dr. Pankhurst led a march of hungry men to the Guardians' office, where Emmeline was sitting inside with the other officers.

When the other Guardians refused to hear the deputies of the march, saying it was no concern of theirs, Emmeline stood up and told them, in fiery words, just where their duty lay. From that time on they stopped making remarks about "our charming lady Guardian" and treating her like a pretty idiot. Emmeline had no objection to compliments, but she wanted to be considered a serious Guardian, not just an ornament to the board.

In the evenings, after meetings of the board, she returned home aglow with battle fire. Usually she found her husband in his favourite chair by the fireside, reading or making notes on some legal case, with the children grouped around him studying their school lessons. Emmeline would enter this quiet scene like a whirlwind, hardly stopping to take off her coat or loosen her hatpins before plunging into her exciting tales.

"They are infuriating, those men!" she would exclaim. "They care nothing, really, for those in the poorhouse or for the aged or the orphans. The poor old men and women have no chairs to sit on, only benches without backs to them. The women haven't even any pockets in their gowns, so they can keep any little treasure or bit of needlework with them. All they are allowed to do is sit listlessly all day with no occupation for their hands or minds. And the orphans!"

Now her hat was off and her gloves were stripped from her hands, and she moved over to the fire to warm herself. The children listened to her, dazzled, as other children might listen to stories of a fairy princess and dragons. She *was* their princess. They loved their father, but they adored and worshipped their mother.

Dr. Pankhurst smiled. "And what of your orphans?"

"Can you imagine little girls of seven years of age scrubbing the stone floors of the orphanage, dressed only in one thin cotton frock? In this freezing winter? I found they were not even given nightdresses to sleep in. Matron said she was too modest to mention such a thing as nightdresses to the men on the Board. I shall change all that, but it won't be easy. The Board is much more concerned with economy and keeping down the poor tax paid by their friends, the house owners of the district."

The tea was brought by the maid and placed before her, and while she poured it she was busy answering questions.

The children asked as many as her husband did. Even five-year-old Harry seemed to understand that he would have to share his mother with her "orphans." He had too sweet a nature to show jealousy, but she noticed that he stood close to her chair, touching her whenever he could.

She was proud that he was a big boy, though slender like herself. Throughout all his babyhood she had watched over him anxiously, because she had lost one son before Harry was born. Little Frank had lived only four years when, in 1888, he had been stricken with diphtheria and had died.

All her four children, she thought, were healthy—and happy. She and her husband had resolved that they would not make the usual mistakes with their children that most families of that time did: treating the only son as a real person and the girls as dolls. As soon as they were old enough to understand, Dr. Pankhurst lectured them all on their duties to people less fortunate than themselves and on their responsibilities to rid the world of injustice.

They went to meetings with their parents. They handed out leaflets at those meetings and were encouraged to ask questions afterwards about what had gone on. They learned that some people were too rich while others were too poor, and that there were men and women and children working twelve hours a day for shillings while others spent thousands of pounds on fine carriages and clothes. Especially they learned how unjust it was that men should make all the laws, for women to obey.

They were a tight-knit family. It sometimes crossed Emmeline's mind that, except for the outgoing Christabel, her children had no friends but themselves, and that little Harry might be better off in boisterous play with other boys than always surrounded by females and a father almost sixty years old, but she dismissed the thought as quickly as it came. The Pankhurst children were not ordinary children. That was as it should be. Neither their father nor mother were ordinary.

In five years' time Emmeline altered the whole situation in the Chorlton charity for the better. The workhouse, the poorhouse, the aged and the orphans had warm clothing and good food, yet the institutions were run more economically and without waste. There were comforts for the inmates and even such astounding luxuries as a gymnasium and a swimming pool.

Her name was frequently in the Manchester newspapers. Although she was forty in 1898, she was just coming into the full stride of her vitality and powers. She was so full of life and work that she did not notice that Dr. Pankhurst's health was failing.

He did not even protest when she decided, in June of 1898, to take seventeen-year-old Christabel to Geneva, Switzerland. An old friend of hers, Naoémi Rochefort-Dufaux, whom Emmeline had first met while they were girls together at the Paris finishing school, was now living in Geneva, and it was arranged that Emmeline and Naoémi would exchange daughters for a year.

But after only a few glorious days in Geneva Emmeline was stunned to receive a telegram from her husband. "Please come home. I am not well," it read. She left Christabel in Naoémi's charge, and hurried back to England.

She was too late. In the railway carriage from London to Manchester another passenger opposite her was reading a newspaper, and on the back page Emmeline saw a story with her husband's name in it, bordered in black. She made a wild exclamation, begged for the paper and, while the tears ran down her cheeks, read of his death.

She was stricken with more than grief—with fury, as well. The newspaper editor made much of Dr. Pankhurst and quoted eminent statemen and legal figures to praise the "great doctor" and the "splendid humanitarian" and to exclaim over the terrible loss his death would be to the nation. But what, she thought, had those statesmen and those editors ever done for him when he was alive? Nothing.

Emmeline's emotions, whether for joy or grief or anger, were always powerful ones, and she saw no reason to conceal them. When she reached home she was nearly in a state of collapse, and in no condition to comfort the broken-hearted Sylvia or the bewildered younger ones, Adela and Harry. Rather, it was they who had to comfort her.

The maid, Ellen, who thought Mrs. Pankhurst the most wonderful person in the world, had made that plain to them. They must be good children and not cry; they must think of their mother and not of themselves. So they sat huddled together, holding on to each other and keeping out of the way, as Ellen helped their weeping mother up the stairs to her bedroom.

It was the same in the days to come. Emmeline had no idea she was failing her children in this crisis. If *she* was unhappy, she said so; she could not understand the shyness of a Sylvia, who would have had to be coaxed to speak of her heartbreak over the death of her beloved father, or realize that Adela and Harry were forbidden to run to her for comfort. Even when Harry fell down and hurt himself, the maid, Ellen, commanded him not to tell his mother about it.

And Emmeline was suddenly so overwhelmed with new responsibilities that she had no time to wonder if the children were lost or lonely. She found she was not only penniless but in debt. Dr. Pankhurst's business affairs were in sad order. The furniture had to be sold, along with his huge library and collection of paintings.

The family had to move to a smaller and shabbier house, at 62 Nelson Street, but Emmeline's brother, Herbert, came to live with them and share expenses.

Then Emmeline had to get a job to support her children. She resigned her elected post and became a paid employee of the Chorlton Board of Guardians, as registrar of births and deaths for the district. The salary paid for this was to support her family for many years.

Unwisely, she also opened another fancy-goods shop, intending it as a means of independence for Christabel and Sylvia. Since Christabel was still in Switzerland (though Emmeline could not afford to take Naoémi's daughter in exchange), Sylvia worked in the shop and hated it. She was thankful when her artistic talents earned her a free scholarship to the Manchester Municipal School of Art, where, for at least half of each day, she didn't have to try selling things to people who didn't want to buy them.

Neither she nor Christabel, when she returned home a year later, complained. This was a dreadful time for their mother. To become a breadwinner when she was past forty, to submit her proud head to the instructions of her employers, to endure the drudgery of a tiring and thankless job, to come home, exhausted, to meet all the responsibilities of the household—as well as to sew and mend and patch and coach Harry at his lessons—were all the burdens Emmeline could bear.

She did not mind work. She only minded that, because she had been born a girl, she had never been taught a good trade or a profession. Her job opened her eyes even more fully to the injustices practiced on women, since she had to register the births of illegitimate as well as legitimate babies.

Over and again she saw the pitiful cases of young girls who came in front of her desk to whisper their stories. The men who had seduced them were not punished. Society did not condemn them, but the poor girls were often banished from their homes by outraged fathers, cast penniless on the world to support themselves and their babies, scorned by a world in which laws were made by men for the advantage of men.

But Emmeline Pankhurst was resolved that her new lot in life would not make her bitter or keep her out of touch with political matters. As her job became routine, she regained her vitality. She kept up with the meetings of the Women's Franchise League, and politicians still visited her and thought her a woman of considerable influence.

It was natural that her interests lay mostly in the cause of woman suffrage. If women had the vote, then women could have independence and good jobs and better education. She lost interest in most of her late husband's other ideals of social justice, though she followed his pacifist teachings and denounced the Boer War when England became embroiled in that.

It was a most unpopular stand to take, and her three younger children suffered for it. Because Adela stood up for her mother, she was called names and struck in the face with a book by a schoolmate. Harry was attacked by his schoolfellows, beaten up and left unconscious in the road, where his uncle found him. Sylvia was a solitary figure at her art school, going her own way without friends.

Only Christabel was still popular. She didn't care one way or the other about the Boer War and saw no reason to bother herself about it. This pretty Pankhurst daughter had astounded nearly everyone by deciding to get a degree in law. She was turned down by Lincoln's Inn in London but was allowed to enroll at Manchester University, taking courses that would lead to a bachelor of laws degree. Being a female, she would never be allowed to practice as a lawyer, but Emmeline encouraged her to go on with it.

Nor was her mother surprised. She had long known that behind Christabel's dainty, doll-like prettiness was a cool, clear, logical brain.

All four children were becoming personalities. Christabel was Emmeline's favourite, since they were something alike in temperament. Both were outgoing, fearless, quick-speaking, quick-thinking people. When they decided something was right or wrong, they were never tortured by doubts; there were no ifs and buts and maybes. And they both had style and dash and a taste for the romantic.

Harry came next in her affections. She saw him as the perfect little knight he tried so hard to be to her. His childhood revolved around her; he would do anything to please her.

Between Emmeline and daughter Sylvia there was a slight barrier, which the mother tried to overcome but couldn't because she had no understanding of shy and reserved natures. And Adela was still, in Emmeline's eyes, an undeveloped schoolgirl, whose most outstanding trait was a stubborn independence. Both girls were excellent in their schoolwork and that mattered most, and their mother did not worry much about them.

That both Sylvia and Adela might be jealous of Christabel was something Emmeline half-admitted to herself. It couldn't be helped. She did like Christabel best.

In 1901 Sylvia won the Lady Whitworth scholarship for the best woman art student. In 1902 she won the National Silver Medal for design in mosaics, the Primrose Medal, the Proctor Travelling Scholarship and the National Scholarship to a fine school in London. It was a great sweep of prizes for one girl. It upset the family when Sylvia had to leave home that year and go to London, but her father's friend Keir Hardie kept an eye on her there.

Emmeline was proud, but she was also feeling desolate. Adela had declared her intention of becoming a school teacher. Emmeline saw ahead of her a future where all her children would leave home and scatter, with no central interest to bind them together. What did the future hold for her but loneliness and an obscure job just to keep a roof over her head?

The woman suffrage movement at that time was at a low ebb. The Women's Franchise League, tied in with the Liberal Party, was nothing but an appendage to politicians. The women of Britain seemed no more interested in their own rights than were the men who denied rights to them.

It was at this point that Christabel, who had shown no interest in suffrage, suddenly changed into a fiery crusader. Not only did she change but so did the whole direction of life for the Pankhurst family, because she had thought of the way—the *only* way, as she and Emmeline agreed—to achieve voting power for women.

~//~ Chapter two

As Emmeline listened to Christabel explain her idea, it was as if she heard the echo of her husband's voice—"why don't you *force* us to give you the vote?"—because that was the essence of her daughter's thinking.

"We need a new organization," said Christabel, standing in the centre of the small sitting room and addressing her family. "One that will act boldly and go out and talk to women and convince them it is their right to have the vote. The league and all the other woman suffrage organizations are either too polite or too tied in political parties to act with independence. Politicians just take advantage of us. If we'll work for their elections, they promise to bring into the House of Commons Father's bill for franchise—but do they do it? Never."

"Mr. Hardie does," said Adela.

But Christabel brushed aside the interruption. "He is one man, and he hasn't the power to do much for us. What we need is an organization *of* women *for* women, one that will lead all the women of Britain into militant action. There are millions of women, and if they speak with one voice they will get the vote. But our organization must have no other purpose but that. We must drive, single-minded, to achieve that one purpose and no other—the vote. And with the vote we will raise women to equality in work and in education and before the law!"

Emmeline felt herself alive with excitement. Her mind went leaping ahead. "Oh, Christabel is right, I know she is! I am tired of waiting, tired of having men tell me to be patient, fobbing me off with promises that are never kept. Why should men give us something when we haven't the strength to demand it?"

"But what about all the other reforms Father wanted?" asked Adela.

"First things first," replied her mother. "Once women have the vote and can be elected to Parliament, they will be in a position to make all kinds of reforms. Christabel's plan is superb—and you know why? Because it is so simple. It has the virtue of simplicity. Women who are divided among themselves on other matters can join an organization that calls for only one thing, for suffrage. Women of all ranks of society, from the educated and wealthy to the uneducated working woman, can join together in a crusade so clear-cut that all can understand and sympathize with it."

"And another thing," Christabel still had the floor and she was not finished, "is that we must make a noise. We must get into the newspapers. We must be *heard*. We must make men so uncomfortable that they will give us what we want if only to get rid of us."

This made even Emmeline pause and think. Publicity was foreign to women. Nice women, gentlewomen, did

not do things that would attract unfavourable notice in
newspapers or journals. But she met the challenge and
smiled at Christabel. "I've had that sort of notoriety, and
it has not hurt me. I don't think it will prevent women
from joining us. We've been quiet too long."

Surprisingly, Adela agreed. "History books are full of
how men have achieved what they wanted, and they
didn't do it sitting at home. They organized and went
out into the streets; they gathered in mobs before the
Houses of Parliament; they forced governments to give
way to them."

Emmeline started to speak, but stopped. She gave
Christabel an eloquent glance that bade her be still.
Adela must think things out for herself; if she thought
Christabel was trying to persuade her she would very
likely take the opposite view.

The plainest of the Pankhurst girls, resembling her
father more than her mother, Adela was a puzzle to all
of them. Until she was past three years old she had suffered from a disease of the leg and been unable to walk.
She had therefore been a solitary child, sitting and rocking and making up stories to amuse herself. She was not
the least bit shy, like Sylvia, but she liked to think her
own thoughts and make up her own mind.

Emmeline was the only person who had a real influence on her, and sometimes that influence failed. As for
Christabel, Adela seemed to resent her older sister and
rebelled at any direction from her.

"I suppose," said Adela, thoughtfully, staring into the
fire, "that we must cut any political ties with any political party. We have to be free to criticize as well as sup-

port any candidate. But to think we can achieve what we want without the co-operation of men, of leading politicians, is not sensible." Though she was only seventeen, she was apt to speak like an echo of her father, in his scholarly way. "Suffrage can only be granted by Parliament and by whichever political party is in power there. I grant you we can expect nothing from the Conservatives, but we have many friends in the Liberal Party and even more in the Labour members of the House."

"Oh, agreed," said Christabel, impatiently. "But just because the Liberals say they are for woman suffrage they think they can count on our support and keep us quiet. I say they can't—from now on. They'll have to come to us, support us, *do* something for us, before we'll work for them."

Adela slowly nodded, and Emmeline knew she was won over. It was time to get down to practical matters. It flashed through her mind how absurd it was for one widow and two young daughters to be planning an organization that would lead all British women to the winning of the vote—when they didn't know if even one other woman would follow them—but she quickly pushed that thought out of her mind. After all, they were the Pankhurst family and not like any other.

When Christabel and Emmeline worked out the details of the organization, Adela was appalled at their undemocratic ideas, but at last she grudgingly admitted the necessity of them.

There were to be no constitution, no by-laws, no elections. The founders would choose the leadership, and those leaders would be permanent ones. Their orders must be obeyed without question; their instructions would be binding upon everyone.

"If the membership doesn't like it, they can leave the organization as easily as they can join it," declared Christabel. "We aren't building a political party, we're building an army. Generals in an army don't waste time discussing with privates how the battle is to be waged, and neither shall we."

But it was Emmeline's argument that convinced Adela. "You've seen for yourself the endless haggling and quarrelling that goes on in every other suffrage group. At every election time they split into factions, and when it is over there is always bitterness because some favourite candidate didn't get chosen. We can't have quarrels. We can't have a divided organization, or we're finished before we start."

Adela capitulated. She also readily approved the conditions of membership, because they would enable working women to join as easily as rich ones. Any woman could become a member by paying a shilling, and there would be no yearly dues demanded. Salaries paid to the leaders would be the bare minimum needed for the work. Any large expenses would have to be paid by donations and gifts, or collections taken up at meetings, but no one was to be forced to give or made ashamed if they could not.

Men could not join, but they would be encouraged to attend meetings and help in any way they could.

Each new member would sign a declaration of adherence to the organization's policy, to work for woman suffrage and to promise she would work for no other group until suffrage was won. Any member could be instantly expelled for disagreeing with this policy, or if she came to a meeting and tried to drag in other causes, no matter how worthy those causes were. No member could ask the others to help her in some particular charity or to work against some particular injustice—not until the cause of suffrage was won.

Not until the last details had been worked out and it was time for bed did Emmeline realize that Harry had sat quietly throughout the whole discussion, saying nothing.

"What do you think, son?" she asked, turning low the wick in the oil lamp and handing it to him to light himself to his room.

"I?" he blushed. "Whatever you think, Mamma. You always know what is right."

The next day Emmeline sent out invitations to all the women in Manchester who were particularly interested in suffrage matters—except for those who were jealous heads of their own organizations. The result was a fairly large gathering at her house.

She had expected shock and disapproval over a new organization and over the rules, and some of the women did express alarm that it should be so autocratic and undemocratic. But she was unprepared, in spite of her natural optimism, for the enthusiasm. It started small, then spread like a wave throughout the room, with everyone exclaiming at once that the idea was brilliant.

Suffrage, and only suffrage! These women, too, were tired of seeing their efforts going for nothing, frittered away without getting one step nearer to their goal. A very few women left, saying they weren't interested, but the majority vied with each other to see who could be the first to find a shilling in her handbag and sign the pledge.

So the Women's Social and Political Union was born.

Mrs. Jacob Bright and Christabel were chosen as leaders, but when Emmeline's name was put forward she quite sincerely objected. One Pankhurst was enough. She held to this for a few months, but when she realized that all the women looked to her for leadership, insisted she take the chair at meetings and would belong only if she were in charge, she gave in.

From the first moment of organization, the members were swept into activities new to them. No longer could they stay cosily in their own homes, holding meetings among themselves. They had to go out to where people were—on street corners, to outside social gatherings or to political meetings—and force themselves to speak about woman suffrage. Timid ladies found themselves standing on stools, while other ladies steadied them, and braving the jeers and laughter of street-corner bullies as they spoke of injustice to women.

Emmeline and Christabel were by far the best speakers, though Adela soon developed an earnest style of her own. Christabel's striking combination of a charming face and figure along with the logic of her legal brain always commanded attention, but it was Emmeline Pankhurst who could quiet the most unruly audience and bring unknown women to her afterwards, with their shillings in their hands.

When men shouted at her: "Go get yourself a husband, and stay at home where you belong!" or "If you had a handful of kids you wouldn't be bothering about votes!" and when conservative women who had paused to listen for a moment, shuddered and said: "What an unnatural female!" she was ready with answers for them. She had been a beloved wife, she was the mother of four children, she held the home together for them and she had nothing but praise for wifehood or motherhood.

"Can you say the same?" she demanded of her hecklers. "Do you honour the mother who bore you, or your own wife, when you deny them what you look upon as a right for yourself? When you treat them as creatures beneath you?"

Membership in the Women's Political and Social Union, or the Union, or the W.S.P.U., as it was often called, grew steadily, by ones and twos and threes. New faces were seen at the Pankhurst home; new, and younger, women began calling to find out what they could do.

From London, Sylvia made her contribution by sending them more of her scholarship money than she kept for herself. At this time in her life she could have broken away from her family and devoted herself solely to art, but she was too emotionally tied to her mother. She often criticized Emmeline, but unwillingly she adored her. Sylvia did not then have the self-confidence to make a new life and new friends; instead, she tried to win Emmeline's favour by denying herself every comfort and living in a miserable room.

Her only London friend was Keir Hardie, who was like a second father to her. When he talked to her of his hard, bitter life as a miner's child and of how much he hoped to do for working people in his seat in Parlia-

ment, Sylvia wondered if her art was not an indulgence
and her duty was to political causes. So she cut down on
food, bought no clothes and sent everything she could to
her mother.

Emmeline was glad of the money, but she had little
idea of what a great sacrifice this was for a twenty-year-
old girl. How could she? To Emmeline, nothing was too
much for anyone to give for the cause of woman suffrage;
no one gave more than she did, herself.

What Christabel did seemed more to the point, because the elder girl was so active, rushing from classes
to meetings. One day she reported to her mother an interesting success.

The Oldham Trades Council of Labour Party men
had arranged a special meeting for Christabel to speak
on woman suffrage to workers in the Oldham district.
After her speech was over, three young girls waited and
asked to talk to her. They were sisters named Kenney,
cotton factory workers, and their spokesman was sister
Annie, small, quick, eager and lively.

Could they join the W.S.P.U.? They handed over their
shillings, but that was not all. Could Miss Pankhurst
come and talk to the women at their factory? They
would make all the arrangements. Christabel agreed to
come.

Christabel had no faith that Annie Kenney knew anything about making suitable arrangements for a meeting,
but when she arrived on the appointed day she was agree-
ably astonished. Annie was a born organizer. She had
talked to the cotton-mill women and persuaded them to
stay late, tired as they were after a day's work; she had

bullied the foreman into giving her a room for the meeting.

It was a success. Almost all the women enthusiastically joined the W.S.P.U. and pledged themselves to talk to others.

The real success was the association between Annie and Christabel, which was to last almost their lifetimes. Every general needs a competent aide, and Annie became that to Christabel. Any young girl as deprived by birth and education as Annie, eager as she was to escape the dreariness of her cotton-mill life, needed an ideal and an idol to inspire her, and Christabel was that to Annie.

Nor did Annie care how little she had to live on if it meant she could become part of the Pankhurst world.

It was she who suggested the next move that would widen the field of suffrage work. A travelling fair, called the Lancashire Wakes, went from town to town through Lancashire and Yorkshire counties. People flocked to the fair. They came for pleasure and fun, but they were also accustomed to speakers from the Salvation Army and other serious groups who gave talks on the sidelines. Why shouldn't the W.S.P.U. do the same?

They did—as often as Emmeline could get away from work, Christabel and Adela from school, or they could persuade other members to take their places. And they found that, in spite of some rough heckling from men who were too full of beer to mind their manners, they attracted larger crowds than anyone.

Emmeline discarded all complicated slogans in favour of the simple one: *Votes for Women!* This was on the banner they held over the speaker's chair and on all the leaflets they distributed. Most of the audience gathered around them as they would for any free and exciting sideshow, but always there were women—and some men —who showed their sympathy and donated some money.

For two years the W.S.P.U. worked and grew, making itself known throughout the two counties and finding that the ripples of their work were spreading even beyond. Letters came to the Pankhurst home from unexpected sources. The newspapers mentioned them, and Christabel pushed hard for publicity—any kind, whether it was favourable or not.

She was developing a shrewd sense of the value of making woman suffrage a thing that was talked about. At night she and Harry would go out and chalk up in bold letters on city pavements notices of meetings or just *Votes for Women!*

Late in 1904 Keir Hardie wrote Emmeline that there was a chance he could introduce Dr. Pankhurst's bill for woman suffrage in the next session of Parliament. Although the Conservative Party still held the offices of Prime Minister and Cabinet, Liberal and Labour Party strength in the House of Commons was growing, and most of those members had promised to support him.

So, in February of 1905, Emmeline got a few days' leave from her job and went to London to help him. Sylvia accompanied her to Parliament and waited with her in the anteroom of the House of Commons. Then Keir Hardie came and explained what would happen. On this Wednesday there would be the usual custom of balloting to see which favourite bills of which members would be permitted to be heard in this session. He was hopeful for a place for the Suffrage Bill.

When he went back into the House, Emmeline did not stand idly by. She sent in her name to various politicians whom she considered her friends or who were indebted to her and Dr. Pankhurst for help given in their elections. When they came out to greet her, she wasted no time in telling them where their duty lay and why they had to support Mr. Hardie.

By now, from all her husband's teachings and from Christabel's legal studies, she knew her facts about the injustices done to women regarding inheritances, property rights and marital status. From her own experiences as registrar and, especially, from Annie Kenney's stories, she also knew that the claim that women were better off under men's chivalry was a pack of lies.

A cotton-mill manufacturer might put his own wife and mother up on a pedestal, but that did not stop him from exploiting the poor women who worked for him. There was no chivalry and no protection there. He worked them terribly long hours, at less pay than men got, with no safeguards for their health.

The whole basis of argument that women should not be treated the same as men because they were too weak in brains and bodily strength was brutally exploded when it came to profits. In mills and factories women slaved alongside of men and were expected to be as fast and capable as men; as much was demanded of them, and far less was given to them.

As Emmeline talked, her cheeks flushed and her eyes

sparkling her daughter marvelled at her. She knew that
her mother's elegant appearance was only made possible
by her exquisite sewing, by borrowing a ribbon from
Christabel and a brooch from Adela, and this did not
surprise her. Emmeline Pankhurst always had a flair for
style. But Sylvia had seen little of her in the past few
years and was unprepared for how young she had grown.

The W.S.P.U. had brought new life to Emmeline. She
did not try to dress youthfully or pretend to be less than
her forty-six years, but there was a zest and excitement
about her that made her daughter feel drab by com-
parison.

When Hardie came out of the House chamber, he was
troubled. He had not won a place; he could not introduce a bill that session, but his good friend Bramford
Slack had won a place for another measure. If Slack
could be persuaded to substitute the bill for woman
suffrage instead of the one he had proposed, he would
have the right to do this.

Emmeline went into a whirlwind of action, dragging
Sylvia with her. Bramford Slack was not to be found at
Parliament, but that did not stop her. She went to his
house and pleaded with his wife, to such good purpose
that that lady persuaded her husband to make the sub-
stitution.

One step had been won, and Emmeline's hopes were
high. Before she left London she got in touch with the
National Union of Women's Suffrage Societies, a committee that tried to co-ordinate the work and bring about
co-operation among all the suffrage groups in Britain.
The National Union was delighted to hear that Mr.

Slack would actually propose votes for women during that session, and promised to do all they could to help.

Friday, May 12, was the day set for Mr. Slack to introduce the measure. It would have to be heard that day and given a preliminary passing for future debate, or it would go by default and he could not speak again.

Emmeline again came to London. When she and Sylvia reached the entrance to the House of Commons, they were overjoyed to see the street and lobby and anterooms crowded with women, many of whom Emmeline already knew. They greeted her with smiling faces. "A great day for us, Mrs. Pankhurst," said little, elderly Mrs. Wolstenholme Elmy, a pioneer suffrage worker, "and we have you to thank for it."

"The battle isn't won yet," warned Emmeline, but her hopes were high.

Those hopes dwindled as the hours dragged on. None of the women had thought to secure seats for themselves in the small section of the House Visitors' Gallery allotted to women, so none of them knew what was happening. Keir Hardie came out to report, and he was worried. Mr. Slack's proposal was to be the last on the day's schedule, and it seemed that discussion of prior bills was being deliberately prolonged. Time was running out.

Emmeline sent in a note to the Conservative Party leader, Mr. A. J. Balfour, threatening him that no woman would work for his party in the next general election unless Slack's bill was heard. It was an empty threat. Most of the women supported the Liberal Party anyway.

There was only one hour, then a half-hour, then ten minutes left. The door of the House opened as Keir Hardie strode out, and behind him Emmeline could hear a roar of laughter from the House chamber.

"It's all over," Hardie told the women, bitterly. "We've lost. They talked the time away, deliberately arguing and laughing about trifles—anything to prevent the bill from being proposed this session."

"I heard them laughing. Were they laughing at *us?*" Emmeline was shocked and furious.

"It amounts to the same thing. They were carrying on a ridiculous argument about tail lights, saying that if a cart had to carry a red light at the rear, why shouldn't a horse have one on his tail? But the real reason for the laughter was that they were enjoying themselves, killing time and mocking us. Grown men acting like children—just to prevent woman suffrage being discussed this session!" Hardie was indignant. "The Liberals were as bad as the rest!"

He had to go back to the House for a moment, but the women were in no mood to go home. Their spirits were sore with resentment. They wanted to discuss what had happened. They left the lobby, but near a statue outside the House of Lords they gathered to talk. Mrs. Elmy, the pioneer who had suffered so many rebuffs, tried to make a speech.

Policemen converged on them. Not even Mrs. Elmy's age and white curls could affect them in what they considered their duty: the women must leave. The police attitude became threatening, but when Keir Hardie appeared—a member of Parliament—they were more polite

and led the women across the street to Broad Sanctuary
in front of Westminster Abbey.

There the women could have their impromptu meeting, and there they passed a strong resolution of protest
to the House of Commons for its shameful actions that
day.

That night, in Sylvia's shabby room, Emmeline paced
up and down as she did when she was agitated, wringing
her hands and venting her feelings in angry denuncia-
tions and tragic exclamations.

"The wretches—laughing at us! When I think of the
promises the Liberal Party made to your father and to
me! Oh, when I think of them, and think how we must
go on enduring such humiliations, year after year—it's
too much! It's more than the spirit can stand . . ." Suddenly, in the midst of her dramatics, she caught sight of
her daughter's face and saw that Sylvia was really suffering. It flashed across her mind that this sensitive girl
truly thought her mother was in despair.

She stopped pacing, laughed and reached out to pat
Sylvia's cheek. "Don't look at me like that. Bless you,
your old mother likes it. This is what I call life!"

It was true. Disappointed as she was, she was in the
centre of a conflict, in the heart of a storm, and that was
life to her. The worse the disappointment, the stronger
she rose to meet the next challenge.

Sylvia could not understand such a temperament, so
foreign to her own. She knew her mother too well to
think that such extravagant behaviour was any evidence
of insincerity, yet she was incapable of matching it with
the same kind of dramatics. The events of the day made

her feel just wretched. Would she ever be the daughter Emmeline wanted?

When Emmeline returned to Manchester she found Christabel knew all about the Parliamentary failure, and her response was the same as her mother's. The Liberals would find they could not get away with this betrayal! Her anger was satisfying to Emmeline, but when she announced her next move her mother was horrified.

"I am going to prison," said Christabel, and hurried to explain before Emmeline could voice her shocked protest. "Annie and I have talked it all over, and we have decided it is the only way to call public attention to the Liberals' treatment of us—because it will be the Liberals who will put us in jail."

"You are going to get yourself deliberately arrested? Why?" Part of Emmeline's mind was leaping ahead to the significance of the action; part was pulling back, trying to say that this must not happen to Christabel.

Quickly, Christabel outlined her plans. A nationwide general election was coming up. The Liberal Party intended to make a strong bid to take over the Government. A great meeting was scheduled in the Free Trade Hall of Manchester, where the Liberals would launch their campaign and throw down the gauntlet to the Conservatives.

Christabel and Annie would be at that meeting.

If they were allowed to speak and present the case for woman suffrage, well and good. But if not, they were resolved to make a disturbance that would get them sent to jail. The newspapers would be full of it. Then let the Liberal leaders answer to the women who supported them why they had sent a daughter of Dr. Pankhurst, one of the Liberal Party founders, to jail!

Emmeline listened. The plan was good. But she said: "I shall go with Annie—not you, Christabel."

"The plan wouldn't work with you, Mother. They wouldn't dare arrest you, not in Manchester. They wouldn't let you speak, but they would be polite and shut you up," said her daughter. And Emmeline had to admit that it was true.

On the night of the meeting the two girls were gay and full of little nervous jokes, and Emmeline tried hard to answer them in the same spirit. She teased Annie about the bulge under her coat, where she was carrying a rolled-up banner which read "Will You Give Votes to Women?" She even smiled as Christabel walked out the door and laughingly called back to her mother: "We shall sleep in prison tonight!"

Then Emmeline was left alone in her private agony. Her favourite child was going into danger, and all she could do was wait and pray through the long and miserable hours.

This was something she would have to face, not only for Christabel but for her son and other daughters. If love for them made a coward out of her, she would be ruthless with that love. She would steel herself to their sacrifice. She would honour them by giving them the same privilege she demanded for herself, of suffering for a cause they all believed in.

Otherwise, in some crisis, she might weaken and falter, try to hold them back and thus fall back herself.

⌒⫻⌐ Chapter three

Harry and Adela wanted to stay up with her, but she sent them to bed and waited alone. It was nearly midnight when the door opened and there were Christabel and Annie, their eyes dancing with excitement. Emmeline's first thoughts were that nothing had happened, but she was quickly informed that it had.

Both girls were talking at once. "We did it!" "Christabel did it—she got us arrested!" "We're ordered to court tomorrow, to be charged and sentenced."

"What did you do, Christabel, to get arrested?" her mother asked.

The girl blushed. "I *spat* at the policemen."

"You *what?*"

"I had to, Mamma. Let me explain from the beginning," said Christabel, and she did, with interruptions from Annie.

Everything had gone much as they expected at first. They had previously secured tickets to good, prominent seats in the hall, and they had sat quietly in the packed auditorium as speaker after speaker got up to praise the

Liberal Party and outline its platform issues for the coming election.

When the speechmaking was over and only the final words by the chairman were yet to be said, and the girls could be certain that woman suffrage was not going to be mentioned by anyone, Annie had risen to her feet. At the sight of her there was a silence. She had shouted: "Will the Liberal Party give votes to women?" Christabel leaped up and echoed the shout, unfurling the banner as she did so.

It rippled over the heads of the delegates as the two girls held it up for the men on the platform to see, then turned to display it to the audience. And again the girls cried out the same words that were on the banner: "Will the Liberal Party give votes to women?"

The effect was stunning. The hall was in instant turmoil. Men who had been jovially congratulating themselves on their party and their chances of victory were furious that they should be reminded of something they would rather forget. Yells came from all over the hall. "Throw them out!" "Call the stewards and throw those girls out." "Sit down, you girls!" Here and there a man clapped or called out encouragement to Christabel and Annie, but those few were lost and stifled in the general roar of anger.

The men on the platform went into an excited huddle. Neither Annie nor Christabel would be silent; in spite of the boos and yells at them, or the men who were tugging at them to make them sit down, they kept on their feet and kept on chanting for votes for women.

Finally one of the platform figures, who happened to

be Chief Constable of Manchester, was sent down to
speak to them. "If you young ladies will sit down and be
quiet until after the vote of thanks has been made, your
question will be taken up as an entirely proper one. Will
you do this?

"Of course," they told him, and promptly sat down.
Christabel, aware of rules in such meetings, hastily put
their question in writing on a slip of paper and sent it up
to the platform. They would not be able to say she had
not fulfilled all the rules.

But the promise to them had been a ruse. When the
usual vote of thanks to the planning committee was
given, Sir Edward Grey rose to say the final words and
adjourn the meeting, all without one reference to the
question of woman suffrage. Furious, the girls once more
jumped up and broke into Sir Edward's words by unfurling their banner again and shouting out: "Will the
Liberal Government give the women the vote?"

The Chief Constable had gained the time he needed
to summon his policemen. They were waiting outside.
Inside the hall the party stewards rushed to the girls and
dragged them, kicking and struggling, out of their seats
and down the aisle to the exit. As they went, some of the
delegates joined the fray, slapping and pushing at the girls
as they were hustled along. Christabel heard one man
yell, as he punched her in the back: "Suffrage? I'll give
the hussies something to suffer for!"

The trained police took over, pinioned the girls' arms
and frogmarched them so they could not kick or struggle.
It was the obvious intention of the police to get them

away from the hall and then let them go free, but that was not what the girls wanted.

"I didn't know what to do," confessed Annie, her eyes shining with admiration for the clever Christabel. "You have to resist to be arrested, and they were holding us so we couldn't resist . . ."

"So," said Christabel, "I resisted the only way I could. I could only turn my head, so I spat at them. Oh, not really. My mouth was too dry. I just puckered it up and made the motion. But the officer understood immediately what I was doing and that I knew the law. It was 'technical' assault upon him, and he was forced to acknowledge it and order us taken to the police station."

"And there," Annie interrupted, "we were booked and ordered to return tomorrow for our sentence. Mrs. Pankhurst, if we are given our choice of paying a fine or going to gaol, you must let us go to gaol."

Through Emmeline's mind there came a sudden vision of tomorrow's newspapers with the headlines "Pankhurst daughter gaoled for spitting," and she was thankful her dignified husband was dead and spared the humiliation. But she let nothing of this show in her face and smiled steadily as she promised, "Yes, you can go to gaol, and—oh, I am proud of you!"

Annie and Christabel spent five days in prison. It was a lark for them, in spite of the cells and the prison uniforms and the unpleasant food. The prison matron did not know what to make of such odd "criminals," and she treated them with consideration.

The real ordeal was Emmeline's. The Manchester

newspapers did indeed headline the arrest and prison sentence, and the story was picked up by newspapers all over the country. People sent her the clippings. She had to read severe editorial comment upon a mother like Mrs. Pankhurst who allowed her daughter to indulge in such disgraceful behaviour, or stories that mocked the girls and what they had done.

She was interviewed by newspaper reporters, which pleased her because she was able to tell them exactly why the W.S.P.U. had resorted to this action. She was visited by old friends in the Liberal Party, who remonstrated with her for allowing Christabel to disrupt a serious meeting. To them she said, when they protested that Dr. Pankhurst would have been sorry to see his daughter act as she did, "Dr. Pankhurst once told me we women should scratch your eyes out and force you to give us the vote—and perhaps we are ready to do just that."

Threats were made that she would lose her job, and if she had not been so competent in it she might have been fired. The threat came to nothing.

Hardest of all for her to answer were the pleas of old friends who came to offer to pay the girls' fines and get them out of jail. She had to shock them by refusing. She had to tell them the publicity was just what the W.S.P.U. wanted, and it was already doing some good.

Responses were coming to her from women all over the British Isles. The letters told their own pitiful stories of women under the tyranny of laws made by men for men. One woman wrote that she had left a domineering husband, started a shop and prospered in it, only to have him walk in one day and take it away from her. The law gave him that right.

Others told of education denied them. Unmarried daughters were scorned; they were the slaves of their parents or became governesses to other people's children and treated with contempt. Married women sent Emmeline their shilling for membership, but asked her not to write them since their husbands would open any letter. That was their right.

Emmeline could feel a stirring in these women, a reaching out from behind their cages.

When Christabel and Annie were released one morning and came home, they brought with them just such a woman as Emmeline had been thinking of. She was Mrs. Flora Drummond, who had read of the arrest and had waited outside the prison every day to meet them.

Emmeline took to her immediately, recognizing in her a powerful ally. Mrs. Drummond had the square, short build and the homely, pug-nosed face of an army sergeant-major, but with it went a jolly, self-assured manner that was most appealing. She joined Emmeline in giving the girls a good breakfast, and told them her story.

She was married to a man who was habitually in and out of work, and it was she who supported them both by her job with the Oliver Typewriting office. Her air of self-assurance was later to earn her the nickname of "General" Drummond among the W.S.P.U. workers, but no one knew better than she that she was only a captain under the Pankhursts, and glad of it.

She was a good organizer, in her blunt way, with no

patience for haggling over trifles. But it was as a rough-and-tumble speaker that she excelled. The first time Emmeline saw her standing on a chair and addressing a street-corner meeting she knew the Union had a find in Mrs. Drummond. Far more than the ladylike Pankhursts, she could jolly a hostile crowd until she had their sympathies, or give a persistent heckler as good a roasting as he was giving her.

"Who changed your nappies for you when you were a lad?" she would cry to a heckler. "A woman did. Who brought you up to be a gentleman?—which you aren't, no fault of hers. Who married you and bore your children and gave you love and devotion?—which you don't deserve. A woman. Yet you say they aren't good enough to share the vote with you. Be off, before I take my brolly to you!" And she waved her umbrella at him as the heckler slunk away.

Another active W.S.P.U. member, a school teacher, Teresa Billington, had arranged a welcome-home meeting for Christabel and Annie when they got out of jail, and dared to hire the Free Trade Hall for it. Emmeline was worried that there wouldn't be enough of an audience to fill it, but she was wrong. The place was crowded.

The girls' daring act had stirred women who had never made a move before. Perhaps they felt that the suffrage movement was at last getting somewhere, and they wanted to join it. A newspaper had coined a new name for the girls, and before the meeting was over everyone in the hall was enthusiastically calling themselves by that name—"suffragettes."

The membership of the W.S.P.U. trebled in the com-

ing months. There was a stir all over the country. It
was action that had been lacking in the movement before; it was action the W.S.P.U. promised, and it was
action that women wanted. Mrs. Wolstenholme Elmy
deserted her old suffrage organization in London to join
the W.S.P.U. and brought with her the dynamic Nellie
Alma Martel, who was distinguished as much for the
jewels she wore everywhere as for the brilliance of her
mind.

With so much more to do, Annie Kenney quit her job
at the mill and moved into the Pankhurst home. Emmeline's brother, Herbert, obligingly gave her his room and
departed, saying good-naturedly that there was too much
uproar in the house for him.

Sylvia came to Manchester for a short vacation and
was immediately plunged into the work. A young politician named Winston Churchill was to speak for the
Liberal Party, and Sylvia was sent to disrupt the meeting.

She managed to sidle, unnoticed, right up to the platform, and when Mr. Churchill paused for breath during his speech she called out: "How do you stand on
votes for women?" Churchill was outraged; the stewards
rushed forward, grabbed Sylvia roughly, bundled her
out of the hall and locked her in an anteroom.

She proved herself resourceful. She managed to climb
out through a tiny window and went right back into the
hall and down the aisle to confront an astounded
Churchill with the same question.

Emmeline was pleased with her, and Sylvia was amazed
at herself. True, she had been in agonies of shyness before she had risen to her feet in the hall, and she had a

terrible headache from nerves when it was all over. But while the excitement was going on she had been swept along with it, exhilarated by it.

"Christabel and I are the politicians of the family," Emmeline told her. "You are the artist." But Sylvia told her, timidly: "Perhaps I can be both."

Money trickled into the W.S.P.U., but only in small amounts, and they were always hard pressed. The handling of finances was a slapdash affair. Theresa Billington kept the books, but the spending was Emmeline and Christabel's decision. They gave it out as the need arose —for trolley fare for a speaker, for the calico and paints for banners and for leaflets and pens and ink. They even gave what they could to help Keir Hardie in his election.

No one questioned how they spent the money. People had only to look at the Pankhursts' shabby clothes to know nothing was spent on themselves. Emmeline even squeezed a little for the W.S.P.U. out of her small earnings, and the house was the Union headquarters. The parlour and dining room were filled with tables and desks, and there was a constant coming-and-going as women and girls made banners, typed letters, wrote leaflets or held meetings.

With Christabel still in law school, Sylvia back in London completing her art studies, Adela in training to be a school teacher and Harry, now seventeen, getting his education by fits and starts, Emmeline felt she had her hands full, especially since the W.S.P.U. took every moment of free time. Harry particularly worried her. He looked strong, but he wasn't, nor was he doing well at school. She had been told he needed eyeglasses, but

comfortable inside their homes? If they did come, would they agree to march to Westminster in that rain?

She took her seat on the platform and tried to count up how many women were in the audience. It was a poor showing. Perhaps there were a hundred or so scattered in the seats of the hall. But just then there was a commotion at the door. It was pushed open, and there was Sylvia, her face flushed and triumphant. Behind her there marched in, laughing and singing and making light of their drenched clothes, some four hundred women from the East End.

And more came, by ones and twos from all over London, until Caxton Hall was almost filled. Even the fact that they had braved the rain added to the feeling of exhilaration; they had already shown they were ready to dare anything.

Emmeline got to her feet to make her speech and was greeted with thunderous applause. She was amazed that her name and reputation seemed as well known here as in Manchester. But she had not relied solely upon herself to stir this audience. One of her most outstanding talents for leadership was her sure sense for drama and theatrical effects.

The only other speakers on the platform were Annie Kenney and Mrs. Drummond, and Emmeline had picked them for their contrast as much as for their speaking ability.

She had insisted that Annie dress in the same clothes she wore as a cotton-mill worker, with plain cotton skirt and blouse and wooden clogs on her feet. And on her other hand was Flora Drummond, neither too young nor

too middle-aged, stout and bustling and homely. In the
centre was Emmeline herself, elegant in spite of her poverty, still beautiful in spite of her years and hard struggles.

Everyone in the audience could identify with one or
the other on the platform. Every woman could feel this
was her crusade, not just for the young or the old, the
rich or the poor.

Emmeline spoke, then, of what the vote would mean,
not only to women but to the whole nation. With the
vote, as full citizens, women could be elected to Parliament and there they could right wrongs, change unjust
laws and sweep away all the restrictions that were now
depriving Britain of the brains and talents of half its
people—its women. She promised the audience that the
W.S.P.U. would no longer submit to tyranny. They
would no longer be silent. They were prepared to take
any action necessary to force their demands upon the
Government.

At this there were cheers throughout the hall. She had
to hold up her hand to quiet them, and remind them it
might not be necessary. The new Government had promised to bring in a woman suffrage bill, and she hoped
they would.

Annie spoke next, going into more detail about the
rules for membership and the aims of the W.S.P.U. She
was halfway through her speech when there was an interruption. Sylvia came to the platform to whisper to
her mother.

Immediately Emmeline rose again, put her hand on
Annie's arm to silence her and then announced that the

King's Speech had just been read to the two Houses of
Parliament and in it there was not a single mention of
woman suffrage!

(The King's Speech might or might not be read by
His Majesty, but the content of it was actually the programme for the coming year by the new Government of
the Liberal Party.)

There was a murmur of outrage, then silence in Caxton Hall. Into that silence Emmeline said she would call
this meeting adjourned as of now, and would lead a
procession to Parliament.

"Who will go with me?" she asked.

All the hundreds in the Hall surged to their feet and
responded, "We will!" In spite of the rain and the cold,
the whole audience formed in a wide, undisciplined line
behind Emmeline, Mrs. Drummond, Sylvia and Annie,
and as they went down the street they filled it from curb
to curb. Umbrellas bobbed over their heads, but nothing
could save their long skirts, brushing the pavement, from
becoming soaked through.

The rain did them one good turn. There were fewer
people driving in the streets or walking on the pavements
to impede their march. The few passers-by stared at them
in wonder or asked where they were going; a few drivers
of horse-drawn cabs or carts shouted at them to get out
of the way, but not even a policeman tried to stop them.

Not then. However, the news of their coming had
sped ahead of them, and at the Strangers' Entrance to
the House of Commons a line of police were stationed
in force. The officer in charge informed Emmeline that
the women could not go in. The entrance was closed.

The women would not leave. Word of their demonstration outside was brought into the House chamber.
Keir Hardie immediately launched into an impassioned
speech, demanding that they be let in to speak for themselves. At last the Speaker of the House relented and
said they could come in, in delegations of twenty at a
time.

The first twenty went in, with Emmeline as their
spokesman. Afterwards she went outside and waited
while, slowly, the hundreds of women got their turn
to enter the House chamber and make their plea for the
right to vote.

Never had she felt such pride in women and such
contempt for men.

The patient women standing in the long line were
soaked to the skin and chilled to the bone before they
could enter the building. And as Emmeline looked at
their blue-pinched faces and wet, bedraggled clothing,
she thought of the contrast inside: members of the House
lounging comfortably on their padded benches, warm
and smug, listening to the delegations with amused or
indifferent faces, whispering among themselves. A few,
not troubling to hide their boredom, leaned back to read
their newspapers.

Couldn't they sense, as she did, the strength and courage of these women? What the women were doing seemed
so dismally futile, but it wasn't. They were acting. They
were stalking the lion of the Government in his own den.
With such women as these, Emmeline thought, in time
a mighty force could be built to bring that lion down!

The next day Keir Hardie brought two very special

people to Emmeline, two leaders for the great army of
her vision. They were Mr. and Mrs. Pethick-Lawrence,
a handsome, distinguished couple. Emmeline was drawn
to them from the first moment she saw them, and they
to her.

Mrs. Lawrence was a lovely-looking woman, only a few
years younger than Emmeline, but wealth had shielded
her from the hardships of life and she looked more youthful than her years. By odd coincidence, her name too
was Emmeline.

Her husband had also come from a wealthy family,
and could have had a brilliant career in politics or science. He had made a splendid record both at Eton and
at Cambridge University, where he had been President
of the Union, the debating society, and won honours both
in mathematics and natural sciences and prizes in law
and political science. He had his degree in law and was
a barrister. In his early days he had been a Conservative,
and considered by them worth grooming for a seat in
Parliament.

But his liberal views had ripened, and he had with-
drawn his candidacy and was devoting his life and money
to helping the poor and unfortunate. He and his wife
had formed a co-operative dressmaking society to give em-
ployment to women, and had built a holiday hotel for
working girls and a children's cottage at their country
home. Mr. Lawrence had founded a daily newspaper,
the *Echo,* and a monthly paper, the *Labour Record,* and
through that they had met Keir Hardie.

Now they were turning their interests to woman suffrage. They had investigated the National Union of

Women's Suffrage Societies, led by Mrs. Millicent Fawcett, but they preferred the more militant methods of the W.S.P.U.

"Mrs. Fawcett," they told Emmeline, "is a fine woman but a cautious one. Education is her weapon, or petitioning Parliament, and she is shocked by your daughter's going to jail. We aren't. We think it brave and necessary if we are to break the conspiracy of silence placed on woman suffrage."

"I admire Mrs. Fawcett, too," said Emmeline. "There's room for more than one suffragette organization. I don't care which one women join, so long as they do join." She was truly large-hearted enough not to care, and her answer greatly pleased the Pethick-Lawrences.

Mrs. Pankhurst told them of her largest problem, that she must spend most of her time in Manchester just when the movement was catching fire in London. Her new friends immediately offered a solution. They would set up a permanent office headquarters in London and pay the rent; they would start a suffragette newspaper; they would be her deputies and business managers for the W.S.P.U. in London.

Gratefully, Emmeline immediately appointed Mrs. Pethick-Lawrence as treasurer of the Union and Mr. Lawrence as business manager (although, as a man, he could not be a member). Before she left again for Manchester they had rented a place at Clement's Inn and had named their embryo newspaper simply *Votes for Women*.

Emmeline took the train with a light heart. The London W.S.P.U. was in good hands.

She came back again in May of 1906 when Keir Hardie

wrote that he had forced the House to debate the question of woman suffrage and he wanted her there on the scheduled day. This time she and Mrs. Pethick-Lawrence and others had seats in the Ladies' Gallery, where they could hear the debate.

That gallery was itself an insult to women. Men visitors to the House sat in the open, but the women were screened from view by a heavy metal grille in front of them. The women had to peer through the holes of the grille. The House members below were thus spared the awful sight of female faces in this sanctum reserved for men.

The debate was also an insult. In spite of Hardie's strong and fine arguments, only a few others dared support him. Most of the speakers—solemn, bearded men—rose to declare that their very admiration for the purity and higher spiritual quality of women made it intolerable that they should subject women to the sordidness of politics. In their roles as wives and mothers women reigned. To give them the vote and elect them to public office would demean them.

From solemnity the debate changed to hilarity. Speakers got to their feet to present an amusing picture of what it would be like if women were elected to office. A woman as Chancellor of the Treasury, when the pretty little things couldn't add on their fingers? Mrs. Pankhurst as the first Lord-Lady of the Admiralty? It was too funny to think about, and the House roared with laughter.

Behind the grille the women cried out in protest and called "Shame!" Police were standing by, ready for this, and they pulled the women out of their seats and pushed

them down the stairs to the lobby. There they heard
that the debate had talked the time away and Hardie's
resolution was defeated.

Leaders of other suffrage organizations were there, and
they turned their disappointment on to Mrs. Pankhurst.
If her group had kept quiet in the Ladies' Gallery and
not created a disturbance, perhaps the debate would have
ended otherwise and their supporters in the House might
have prevailed. Emmeline was not fooled, and she told
them so. The House of Commons had no intention of
voting on Hardie's resolution.

Nor should the others think that just the Conservatives were against them. The Liberals who had sat silent
were just as much to blame.

This was Christabel's thinking, too. In that year the
oldest Pankhurst daughter got her law degree, tying for
top place in her class. She was free to go to London to
work full time for the W.S.P.U.

And the fur began to fly.

~⁄~ Chapter four

The first consequence of her arrival in London was a tiff with Sylvia.

"Don't think," said Christabel, "that we don't appreciate your work in the East End and the support of those women. But we need other kinds of women, with important names, those belonging to important families."

"That's snobbery!" flashed Sylvia.

Her older sister did not deny it. She shrugged. "The newspapers won't mention a Mary Jones from the East End, but they will a Mrs. Pethick-Lawrence, don't forget. Besides, you and your group are too much tied in with Hardie and the Labour Party, and we don't want ties with any political party at all."

"How can you say that?" asked Sylvia. "The Labour strength in Parliament is growing, with more than twenty new members this election. With Keir Hardie as their leader, they are pledged to help us."

"So they say," answered the cool-headed Christabel, "but they have to think of their voters, and a labouring man is no more willing to give his wife equality than the richest Conservative is. It's my policy not to link the

W.S.P.U. to Labour or Liberal or Conservative, and let
me remind you that I'm an officer of the W.S.P.U. and
you are not."

That was that. Sylvia had her choice, to disagree with
Christabel and be pushed out of the Union or yield to
her and stay in. She stayed in, though she never lost her
connection with the women of the East End. These working women always formed a large part of the audience
at any W.S.P.U. meeting or demonstration.

Emmeline liked the new type of women Christabel
attracted: such women as the well-to-do widow Mabel
Tuke, who became honorary secretary of the W.S.P.U.;
Mrs. Charlotte Despard, whose younger brother was
Field-Marshal Sir John French; and Mrs. Cobden Sanderson, of a renowned diplomatic family. Women like
these gave the W.S.P.U. prestige.

Christabel was installed in a room of her own at the
Clement Inn's headquarters. The Pethick-Lawrences became as fond of her as if she were their own daughter,
and she soon took over the writing of most of the editorials for *Votes for Women.*

"Deeds, not words!" was Christabel's rallying cry in
that newspaper. Energetic and imaginative, she stirred
the London women to the kind of activity she was accustomed to in Manchester. They held street meetings. They
canvassed stores to persuade merchants to advertise in
Votes for Women. They handed out leaflets on busy street
corners. At every political or social gathering they were
expected to bring up the question of votes for women.

Christabel also thought of large-scale public appearances. After one disappointing meeting with the Prime Minister, Sir Henry Campbell-Bannerman, she quickly organized open-air speeches in Trafalgar Square in the heart of London. There, thousands of people stopped by to hear Mrs. Pankhurst and Keir Hardie and others tell them what the Prime Minister had said.

"Be patient," he had counselled them. "But we will not be patient!" Emmeline cried out in Trafalgar Square. "We have been patient long enough!"

The throngs of people listening—the curious, the amused, the hostile or the sympathetic—walked away talking to each other of woman suffrage. All London was awakening to the cause of woman suffrage, whether they approved or not. And what was thought of and spoken of in London was carried by newspapers to all parts of Britain.

At the opening of the 1906 autumn session of Parliament a large delegation from the W.S.P.U. crowded into the lobby of the House of Commons. They made such persistent efforts to see the Prime Minister that the police were called in. There was a certain amount of pushing and shoving; in the midst of it Emmeline fell to the floor.

It had been an accident. She wasn't hurt; she could have got quickly to her feet. Her sense of theatrical timing, however, warned her to stay where she was, with two burly policemen standing over her. The picture of her, prone and helpless, bullied by police, had just the effect she wanted.

The women in the delegation were enraged. They were more determined and they pushed harder, ducking

under the arms of the police to reach the door of the
House. The only way the police could break up the turmoil was to make arrests.

Mrs. Pethick-Lawrence, Mrs. Howe-Martyn, Mrs. Cobden Sanderson, Annie Kenney, Teresa Billington, Mary
Gawthorpe and Adela (who happened to visit London
in time for this delegation) were taken to the police station, charged and tried for disturbing the peace and
sentenced to six weeks in gaol. While the trial was going
on, Sylvia made a speech on the steps of the court house,
was arrested and joined the others in the Holloway Gaol
for Women.

The suffragettes made the front pages of the newspapers. The names of Mrs. Pethick-Lawrence and Mrs.
Cobden Sanderson were important enough for feature
stories about them and their suffragette activities.

Christabel's editorials kept the attention to London's
first women gaol martyrs at white-hot pitch. The sales of
Votes for Women leaped upwards. Thousands of leaflets
were printed, asking why these women were in gaol. Were
they criminals? Was a request to see the Prime Minister
an act of lawbreaking?

There were, of course, women as well as men who
read those leaflets and were scandalized that suffragettes
could do anything so improper which would lead to
arrests and gaol, but there were many more who wrote
encouraging letters or who came, shyly, to knock on the
door at Clement's Inn and ask to help. Emmeline encouraged them by instituting the popular "At Homes,"
which were tea parties. She knew well that such a cosy

atmosphere encouraged the timid and made them feel that the suffrage movement was run by ladies.

The tea parties became schools as well. Mrs. Drummond had moved to London, and she and Emmeline and Christabel stood up on chairs and showed how to make street speeches. Or Emmeline acted as if she were at a politician's meeting. While Mrs. Drummond boomed out the usual sort of politician's speech, Emmeline showed how to interrupt at crucial moments.

"My friends—good people," Mrs. Drummond would begin burlesquing a man running for office, "the crucial issue before Britain today is . . ."

"Votes for women!" cried Emmeline.

"Not at all, not at all!" Mrs. Drummond would frown at her. "I'm speaking of our industrial progress. We must give more attention to . . ."

"Votes for women!" cried Emmeline again.

"Steward, throw that woman out of here," demanded Mrs. Drummond, and the tea party rocked with laughter.

When the Holloway prisoners were released from gaol, women crowded the At Homes to welcome them and hear their stories. Mrs. Pethick-Lawrence was a particular heroine. She had suffered in Holloway, but she made light of it. She had no talent for the Pankhurst dramatics, but her straightforward, gentle charm captivated. As soon as the excitement was over, she settled down to work again at Clement's Inn, inspiring others to feel that gaol was no great matter after all. If suffragettes had to endure it, they could.

Under her able direction as Treasurer, with her husband as business manager, the W.S.P.U. was financially sound. The Pethick-Lawrences gave generously of their own money and solicited funds from their wealthy friends. In addition, there were collections from meetings and sales of the newspaper. Expenses were kept to the minimum. Even Christabel, working full time, got a salary of only two pounds, ten shillings a week.

Gone were the slapdash methods of bookkeeping. Accounts of income and disbursements were rigorously kept. The books were regularly audited by a firm of chartered accountants. No one would ever be able to claim that the W.S.P.U. affairs were not honestly run and openly kept.

Adela had got a job as an elementary school teacher but had been fired when she went to gaol. She, too, was then put on the W.S.P.U. payroll, but she was to concentrate her efforts on Manchester and neighbouring towns and cities.

When Sylvia's art scholarship came to an end, it was expected that she would take a paid job with the Union, but she said No. She would support herself by selling artistic wallpaper designs to shops. All her free time would go to the suffrage movement, but Sylvia had no wish to come so directly under Christabel's domination as she would on the W.S.P.U. payroll.

As often as possible Sylvia went to Manchester to see Harry. There was a strong tie between brother and sister —a tie born of their dreamy, romantic, passive natures. But, while Sylvia was forcing herself to become active, Harry was just drifting. At seventeen he still had no ambition, and was happy doing small errands for his mother.

Sylvia spoke to Emmeline of her worries about him, but Mrs. Pankhurst thought such anxiety was nonsense. "He's still growing," she would say. "He's been ill so much that he has all he can do to catch up on his school work. Then he'll find himself."

Emmeline did not see as much of him as she would have wished. She was away from Manchester for longer and longer periods, because she was in demand as a speaker in other cities besides London. She was the best roving ambassador the W.S.P.U. had.

In 1907 she conceived a most audacious idea. When the 1907 session of Parliament opened on February 12, she opened a Women's "Parliament" the same day at Caxton Hall. When the invitation leaflets had been scattered over the city, all London was amused and interested. A Parliament for women—what would that Pankhurst woman think of next?

What she proposed, to the huge audience in Caxton Hall, was that this body send a resolution on women's rights to that "other" parliament in Westminster. The motion was wildly acclaimed; the resolution was approved.

The delegation, led by Christabel, Sylvia and Mrs. Despard, filed out of the hall. The meeting went on, with songs and speeches, until it was interrupted by the sudden return of one member of the delegation. At the sight of her a shocked murmur ran around the hall.

The girl's hair, which had been piled neatly on top of her head under her hat, was now streaming in disorder around her shoulders. Her hat was gone; her jacket was ripped. There was a bruise under her cheekbone. She was trembling as she was helped up on to the platform and turned to speak. "This," she said, "is what the police did to me and the others. They were waiting for us in front of the Strangers' Entrance and refused to let us in. We said we would go in; we had a right to."

The elderly Mrs. Despard had held up the written resolution so the police could make no mistake, and insisted it was the right of any of His Majesty's subjects to present such a resolution to Parliament. She had pushed forward. So had the rest of the women. The police had pushed them away, scattering them, but the women had come back, darting around the police to gain the entrance.

"I saw Mrs. Despard and Sylvia Pankhurst get inside, but they were grabbed," said the girl. "Then the police began arresting people and shoving them into police vans, and I ran back here to tell you."

Emmeline put her hand on the girl's shoulder, moved with her to the front of the platform and showed her to the audience. "This," she said, "is how our Government answers our just and peaceful demands. Even now, some of our delegation are on their way to gaol. Will we let them down?"

Every woman was on her feet. Every voice answered: "No!"

"Will we continue to fight until the Government yields?" Emmeline cried out.

"We will!" answered the women, in the grip of a powerful emotion, blended of fury and determination.

Fifty women and two men had been arrested and

taken to gaol. The next day in court, Christabel spoke
to Judge Curtis Bennett for all of them, declaring that
"our delegation was a perfectly peaceful attempt to present a resolution" and warning him that "there can be
no going back for us, and more will happen if we do not
get justice."

Judge Bennett waved aside any discussion of their
right to present petitions, and scolded the defendants for
the "disgraceful scene" they had caused in front of Parliament. The Government was not to blame. The police
were not to blame. Only the suffragettes were.

He gave out sentences of fines or fourteen days in
prison to most of them—and three weeks in prison to
Mrs. Despard and Sylvia, who had forced their way into
the House lobby.

Not one of the defendants paid their fines. They chose
gaol instead. Again, the newspapers put their pictures
and stories on the front pages. This time some of the
newspaper editorials raised questions that were favourable to the W.S.P.U. Why had the police acted so
roughly? On whose orders? Could it be that the Government was afraid of peaceful petitions? Was the Government becoming alarmed at the strength of the woman
suffrage movement?

The long-suffering Board of Guardians in Manchester
were not so favourably disposed as the newspapers. Mrs.
Pankhurst had gone too far, with her "Parliaments"
and her provocations of the Government. The board
fired her.

It was just as well. With both Christabel and Sylvia
in Holloway Gaol, Emmeline was urgently needed at

Clement's Inn. Her sister Mary stayed on in Manchester
for the time being, to look after Harry and Adela, and
Emmeline became a full-time organizer for the W.S.P.U.
Mrs. Flora Drummond was also now in London, so she
was given an office and secretary at Clement's Inn.

The headquarters expanded to fourteen rooms, with
paid and volunteer workers constantly coming and going.
The new gaolings brought in new members and aroused
old members to fresh activities. All day long they appeared at Clement's Inn to be put to work. They learned
to write leaflets, to type, to add columns of figures; they
distributed leaflets or, with buckets of paste and a brush,
they went out to slap posters up on walls. If there was
no other job for them to do, they grabbed a broom and
swept out the offices.

It was amazing to see wealthy women sweeping out
the office floors, to see a poor, uneducated girl learning
to write letters to branches of the W.S.P.U. in other
cities and to see women who had never ventured before
out of their family circles, addressing the passers-by at a
street meeting. But Emmeline was not at all astonished.

This is what she had felt that day in 1906 when she
had stood in the rain and watched that patient, stubborn
line of women moving past her to enter the House of
Commons. She had sensed that in their dumb courage
there was a fire to be fanned, only needing the sparks to
set it alight. Now it was flaming.

Women of all ages and stations in life wore the
W.S.P.U. buttons or rosettes openly on their coats. They
were proud to be members. And Emmeline and the
Pethick-Lawrences were quick to encourage imaginative

ideas in others. Women vied with one another to think of ways to publicize votes for women, and joyfully reported on their success.

Sunday strollers in fashionable St. James's Park were startled to see a couple of well-dressed women walking down the paths and holding up a banner between them which read: *Votes for Women!* Working girls hung banners from their factory windows. Women used soap to write "Votes for Women" on shop windows in the dark of night.

In all the bustle and excitement at Clement's Inn there was frequent laughter and joking, but no one ever forgot the prisoners in Holloway. Emmeline couldn't forget, not for a moment. Her two daughters were there, and sometimes—in the midst of a conference—she found herself wondering what it was really like to be in gaol.

Mrs. Pethick-Lawrence had made light of it, but she was an exceptionally brave and even-tempered woman. What was prison doing to the arrogant Christabel and the nerve-ridden Sylvia? Emmeline wondered, suffering for them. How would she herself stand up to such an ordeal?

Christabel came out, no worse for it, but furious for every moment she had spent confined, and dramatizing her experiences with the typical Pankhurst taste for theatrics. To Emmeline's great surprise, Sylvia's second gaol experience seemed to help bring her out of her shell. She spoke of prison life at an "At Home" and held her audience spellbound, in a way not even Christabel could.

This was because Sylvia—sensitive and tender-hearted —had genuinely suffered, yet bravely survived, and both her sufferings and her bravery were all the more strongly expressed for the shy and halting way in which she spoke.

Immediately after this Sylvia left London for Glasgow, Scotland, where she could keep an eye on Harry. Mrs. Pankhurst had sent him there because she had at last become disturbed about his health and thought he should be away from school for a while and out of doors. So she had apprenticed him to a housebuilder. Harry would learn carpentering, learn to use his hands and muscles and be doing a man's job in a man's world. Not that his mother wanted him to be a carpenter all his life; she was hopeful he would someday be a lawyer, like his father.

Sylvia took her canvases and paintbrushes with her to make her living in Glasgow. Most of her time, however, was spent in suffrage work; even when she painted, it was the faces of the mill girls who attracted her, or the worn hands of the wives of the fishermen. She saw Harry as often as she could, but, as she wrote her mother, the boy was often too tired to meet her in the evenings.

The letters waited for Emmeline, but it was sometimes a week or more before she saw them. Women all over Britain asked her to come and speak to them, and she went everywhere.

She was not even in London when the second Women's Parliament was held, on March 20, and another deputation sent to the House of Commons. This was a large delegation, led by Lady Harbeton, and it suffered the fate of the preceding one. There was a scuffle with the police, and seventy-five women were arrested and sent to Holloway.

Emmeline had more victims to speak of, more anger to stir in her audiences, more shame to pour down upon the heads of the Government. She had become a superb public speaker. She knew how to hold an audience rapt, how to play upon their emotions, how to move them to tears or lash them to fury.

She went from a home meeting in one town to a large hall in a big city, but her message was the same and the response to her was the same.

By now women everywhere were familiar with newspaper pictures of Mrs. Pankhurst, yet she found the same surprise when they first met her. "What do you expect?" she would ask them as they admired her dress or told her she was beautiful. "A frump? Some odd creature who is doing this work because her mind is twisted?"

From a tour where her popularity and the prestige of the W.S.P.U. had gone up in leaps and bounds, she returned to London to find a rebellion on her hands.

The revolt was led by Mrs. Despard, who resented the autocratic methods of the Pankhursts. The W.S.P.U., said Mrs. Despard, should have a constitution and by-laws, hold elections and have various committees to deal with this matter or that. It was highly undemocratic for all decisions to be made by a few people who had elected themselves to leadership.

"Nonsense," said Emmeline, backing up Christabel. "All that committees do is endlessly argue. We haven't time for that. We haven't time for elections; this is a war and no one elects generals. They are generals because they know what to do and the privates and corporals don't."

Mrs. Despard and her followers left the W.S.P.U., and founded the Women's Freedom League. The great majority of the W.S.P.U. were perfectly satisfied that Emmeline and Christabel knew what was best, and the Pankhursts were enthroned more securely than ever.

No sooner was that settled than Emmeline and Mrs. Martel were off, in the first days of 1908, to a by-election in Newton Abbot, where they helped to defeat a Liberal candidate. The supporters of the defeated man were so aroused that they hunted down the women and finally found them walking in a narrow street. They grabbed Mrs. Martel and began beating her; Emmeline came to her rescue and managed to drag her close to a grocer's shop, whose owner helped Mrs. Martel to safety. But just as the door was closing behind her friend, Emmeline was struck and flung to the cobblestones.

Half fainting, her hands thick with mud from the dirty lane, she looked up and saw the crowd around her. They had found a barrel and were rolling it towards her, to put her into it for sport. Just at that perilous moment she heard the clatter of a horse's hooves, and a mounted policeman came in sight to save her.

She had never thought she could be so grateful to a policeman!

Her ankle had been badly twisted. She was still limping from the injury when the new 1908 session of Parliament opened, and the women countered it again with their own unofficial Women's Parliament in Caxton Hall. Although she had to support herself on the platform by holding the back of a chair, she made light of what had happened at Newton Abbot and much more of a recent experience in Yorkshire, where *one hundred thousand people* had come to a W.S.P.U. open-air meeting!

Emmeline was not a modest woman, but she had never before realized how important she was, personally, to the suffrage cause. It was her name, she had been told, that had drawn those one hundred thousand people, and if that was so, she had a responsibility to them. No general should send troops where she was not willing to go herself. At the Caxton Hall Parliament she announced her intention of leading the deputation that night to the House of Commons in Westminster.

She would be arrested. There were cries of "No—not you!" from all parts of the hall, but she stood firm. Women older and younger than herself had been in prison; it was her turn to go. Women in Caxton Hall wept. They would rather spend weeks in Holloway than think of Mrs. Pankhurst in a cell for one night.

Nevertheless, she went to Parliament, accompanied by Flora Drummond, Annie Kenney and ten others. They wanted to be arrested and tried as political offenders under the Tumultuous Petitions Act, not as ordinary lawbreakers who disturbed the peace. Under the Act, twelve people might present a petition, but thirteen constituted a tumult.

Christabel had widely publicized this action. There were crowds lining the streets, either to sympathize or to jeer at the women, and the police were stationed close to Caxton Hall. They did not stop the deputation, but they ordered the women to walk single file. Even Mrs. Pankhurst, limping, was not allowed assistance on the arm of Mrs. Drummond. She had to walk alone.

The streets between Caxton Hall and the Houses of Parliament had never seemed so long to her, and by the time she reached there she was hobbling and in pain. From all sides of the densely packed pavements came calls of encouragement to the small procession, or jeers and catcalls. "Votes for women!" someone shouted, and was answered by: "Throw them in gaol and let them rot there!"

Turning the corner into the square before the Parliament buildings, Emmeline caught sight of the white face and tear-filled eyes of the young girl behind her—a girl who had never before had people stare and shout at her. "Courage!" Emmeline called over her shoulder. At that moment the police blocked their way and grabbed the nine leading women.

Emmeline's arms were pinioned behind her back, but she struggled and argued. She was bringing a lawful petition to the House of Commons; she had a right to present it.

Her struggles and her words were of no avail. She and Annie Kenney and seven others were arrested, taken to court and released on bail for trial the next morning under the Tumultuous Petitions Act. This was the cheering thing to Emmeline, that for once a suffragette trial would be acknowledged as a political trial.

But the next day those charges were dropped, and instead she and the others were rearrested as common street brawlers. The court had seen the danger in acknowledging that the W.S.P.U. was engaged in a political struggle. It would give too much dignity to their actions.

The trial was a mockery. Police witnesses lied. They said the women had burst from Caxton Hall in a noisy, brawling way, singing and shouting threats, and that they had resorted to vulgar, riotous behaviour when arrested. The judge gave Emmeline and the other defendants the choice of being "bound over"—pledging their word not to commit any further disturbance—or going to prison for six weeks.

They chose prison. They were thrust into a van, along with some male criminals, and taken across London, stopping only once at the men's prison of Pentonville. Was this, Emmeline wondered, what other young girls had had to endure—the lewd and coarse remarks from hardened male offenders?

At Holloway she was lined up in the reception room, where all the women were given a brief physical examination, so superficial that the doctor did not even notice her swollen ankle. Then Emmeline was taken to another room and ordered to strip naked in front of the women warders and put on prison underclothes and a uniform.

She protested. She wanted privacy. The wardress refused, and Emmeline thought of the elderly Mrs. Despard, the young girls, the fastidious Mrs. Pethick-Lawrence, all having to undergo this humiliation, and she marvelled at their courage. Undressing before the hard eyes of the wardress, she thought, was the first move to strip a prisoner of her personality, her pride in herself.

Moving quickly so as to get it over with, she put on the old, coarse undergarments, shutting out of her mind the thought of how many others had worn them before her. They seemed clean. The thick woollen stockings had red stripes, and the shapeless cotton uniform was marked with scattered arrows on it. If a prisoner tried to escape, those arrows would speak of Holloway Gaol to anyone who saw her.

Emmeline was allowed to select unmatching right and left shoes from a basket, given a pair of coarse sheets, a towel, a mug of cocoa and a slice of bread, and ushered to her cell.

She followed the wardress along a passageway. It was as if she was at the bottom of a well. On both sides rose banks of cells, each tier with a narrow corridor running in front of it. Iron steps led upwards, and Emmeline heard her own footsteps clanging harshly on their iron treads; upwards she passed a tier of cells and caught a glimpse of women with their faces pressed against the bars to look at her. A voice came from somewhere, whispering, "Mrs. Pankhurst, are you . . . ?"

"Silence!" ordered the wardress.

Then Emmeline was in her solitary cell. A mattress on a narrow cot, a wooden stool and a bucket—and that was all. The iron door slammed shut behind the wardress, and she was alone. It was terrifying.

Emmeline was not physically afraid, but at that moment she was emotionally a coward. None of the stories she had been told had prepared her for this feeling of becoming a caged animal. She sat, despondent, on the wooden stool and felt a paralyzing fear overtaking her. Her pride was her weakness, she knew. To be humbled was so intolerable she could hardly bear it.

She knew she could have endured this better if some of her dignity had been left to her; if the wardress had addressed her as "Mrs. Pankhurst" instead of "you, there!"; if she could have kept her own dress; if she could have talked to someone, instead of being ordered to be silent.

She took a deep breath, straightened her shoulders, made herself get up and spread the sheets on the bed. The little activity helped, but not much. She tried to eat, but couldn't. And she hardly slept at all that night. Once she had just dropped off in the night when she heard another inmate sobbing. Desolate loneliness swept over Emmeline.

The next day her ankle was so swollen that the doctor was called to examine it. He ordered her into the prison hospital. There the bed was softer, the food was better and she had company. But she found she had only exchanged one horror for another.

In the bed next to hers a young married woman was giving birth to a child. The poor creature pleaded that she was innocent. All night long she moaned of the shame of a child born inside prison walls, and Emmeline was tortured by her sufferings.

Some days later the mother and child were released. The charges had been dropped against her. She *was* innocent. Yet all her life she would bear the stigma of having been in gaol, and of having her child born there.

Emmeline's fury helped her. She had been teetering on the edge of despair. The slowness and the emptiness of the days, with nothing to do and nothing to occupy her mind or hands, had been eating away at her will-power. She had begun to pity herself and cry for no reason at all. The injustice to the young mother roused and stung her.

Clearly she saw what had to be done. Injustice could not be tolerated, even inside prison. It had to be fought against, if only to keep up the suffragettes' spirits. By rights, all suffragettes belonged in the "first division," for political prisoners, where cells were furnished with tables, books, writing materials and newspapers.

Suffragettes would have to demand the rights of political prisoners, and if they did not get them they would refuse to obey prison rules.

Emmeline decided to start the revolt there and then. She demanded paper and a pen to write with. The request was refused, but Emmeline persisted, making such a fuss about it that finally she was brought a slate and a slate pencil.

Oh, the incredible joy of having something to do! The days sped by on wings as she made herself remember every line of French poetry she had learned as a girl, write them down, rub them out and start all over again. As her brain thrived on this activity, her spirits rose.

Now she felt she understood something which had puzzled her before: the attitude of shame that had clung to some suffragettes even after release from prison. Prison did that to them; it made them feel less than human, robbed of their individuality and their pride.

She resolved that this should not happen again to her or to the others. In or out of prison, they would demand certain rights.

~// Chapter five

She was welcomed to freedom by a giant W.S.P.U. rally at Albert Hall. The first thing she saw when she walked on to the platform was the high-backed centre chair with a sign on it that read: "Mrs. Pankhurst's Chair." It had stood like that at every meeting while she was in Holloway, reserved for her and no one else. Tears came to her eyes as she ceremoniously took away the sign, and the audience rose in an ovation to her.

Her own speech was short. She could only say that at last she understood the heroism of those who had suffered gaol before her—particularly those who, unlike herself, had never known hardship in their lives. She honoured them far above herself.

Then Christabel spoke, and Emmeline was surprised at the new note of hope in her voice. Suffrage for women seemed close at hand. Women were showing their strength and power, and the effects were being noticed by the Government. The first large-scale demonstration had been the hundred thousand people who had come to hear Mrs. Pankhurst in Yorkshire. Then there had been other victories.

Winston Churchill had been defeated in an election at North West Manchester by suffragettes because he opposed woman suffrage. True, he had then campaigned in Dundee and been elected to Parliament, but that was a Liberal stronghold and no test for him. He had not dared again to face the women. Mr. Churchill called the suffragettes "hornets."

"And we are!" cried Christabel, to the cheers of the audience.

The Women's Enfranchisement Bill had won a reading in the House of Commons. It was talked out, as usual, but sympathy for the women's cause was growing inside Parliament as well as with the public. The Home Secretary of the Cabinet, Mr. Herbert Gladstone, had made a speech which Christabel quoted:

"On the question of Women's Suffrage . . . argument alone . . . is not enough to win the political day. . . . Then comes the time when political dynamics are far more important than political argument. . . . Men have learned this lesson, and know the necessity for demonstrating the greatness of their movements, and for establishing that *force majeure* which actuates . . . a Government. That is the task before the supporters of this great movement. . . . Of course, it cannot be expected that women can assemble in such masses, but power belongs to the masses. . . ."

"Can we not assemble 'such masses'?" Christabel asked her audience. "Can we not bring tens of thousands of women together?" They called back to her: "We can!"

"Then keep this date in mind," she said. "Midsummer's Day in June, in Hyde Park. We will assemble such masses there as Mr. Gladstone never dreamed of!"

Next, it was Mrs. Pethick-Lawrence's turn on the stage, and again Emmeline Pankhurst blessed the day that had brought this woman to the W.S.P.U. While Emmeline had been in gaol, Mrs. Lawrence had organized a week of self-denial to raise money.

Women had pledged themselves to go without small luxuries of food or clothing. They had organized bake sales and sold the sweets and cakes they had made. Working women had got up an hour earlier in the morning to walk to their jobs and save the trolley fare. Others had sold copies of *Votes for Women*, suffragette booklets or picture postcards of the W.S.P.U. leaders on the streets. The greatest sacrifice of time and dignity had been of those women who had become "street-sweepers."

This was usually the job of ragged little urchins, who earned a penny or two by sweeping street-crossings ahead of pedestrians so they would not get shoes or long skirts muddy. During the week, women had gone out with their brooms and done this job for the cause of woman suffrage.

Now they came to the stage by ones, or by groups, to hand up their pennies and shillings and pounds, and Mrs. Lawrence announced the amounts to great applause. But she had also been busy. She had got autographed books from famous authors and sold them for large sums; she had got thousands of pounds pledged yearly from wealthy sympathizers.

The W.S.P.U. was ready, financially, to support the proposed Hyde Park demonstration on Midsummer's Day.

All that spring the women worked towards it.

Hyde Park Corner, where any speaker was allowed the freedom to stand on a soapbox and say what he or she pleased, had been the scene of many demonstrations in the past. The largest crowd seen there at a political demonstration had been estimated at 72,000 people. The W.S.P.U. hoped, at first, to equal this; then as the response to their calls grew larger, they set their goal at one hundred thousand and upped it to two hundred thousand.

Mr. Pethick-Lawrence took charge. A special office was set up just for this one event. He got the Hyde Park authorities to take out a quarter of a mile of railings, so the immense crowd could spread from the corner into the park itself. He had huge wall posters made, as well as a gigantic map showing how each procession from every corner of London was to march to the rallying point, and had them prominently displayed in London and in other counties.

As women pledged themselves to come, he arranged for thirty special trains to bring them from seventy different towns. Handbills, posters and leaflets poured out of the office; ten great silk banners and five hundred smaller ones were ordered, as well as thousands of flags, in the colours the W.S.P.U. had adopted—purple, white and green.

All sorts of special advertising was resorted to. Buses decorated with signs and flags drove through the streets, filled with singing suffragettes. Theatres allowed them to make announcements during the shows.

It was typical of Flora Drummond that her stunt was

spectacular. She hired a launch and had it sail slowly along the Thames until she was beside the private out-door terrace of the Houses of Parliament, where the members sat with friends to drink tea. Then she un-furled the banner of "Votes for Women"and yelled out: "Come to Hyde Park on Sunday! Hear what the women have to say!"

A police boat chased her launch away, but the audacity of her stunt set all London laughing and talking.

Emmeline was in and out of London during all this time, but mostly out, stirring up the women in the coun-ties. Harry and Sylvia came from Glasgow to London to work day and night, painting posters and signs or chalk-ing up notices on the pavements. They caught only brief glimpses of their mother.

Then the great day came. It dawned clear and sunny, and Emmeline dressed herself for it with trembling hands, so excited was she. She had a new dress, for the first time in two years—a white muslin, the bodice em-broidered by herself with exquisite tiny flowers of purple colour and a narrow purple sash. She and the Pethick-Lawrences went early so they could stand on top of the furniture van, which Mr. Lawrence called their "con-ning tower."

Early as they were, people had already arrived. And as the three stood up in the van they saw the first pro-cession coming down Oxford Street, headed by a four-in-hand coach, and followed by a long, long line of white-purple-and-green-clad women, singing as they came.

Even as the tail of that procession reached Hyde Park and the women fanned out among the trees and walks,

another could be seen coming from a different direction
—then another, and another. Thousands and thousands
of women were marching, and as each passed the van
they saluted or cheered Mrs. Pankhurst. Sylvia led 7,000
women from the Chelsea district; Adela was in the front
of the march from Manchester. Newspaper reporters and
photographers darted in and out or squirmed through
the congested masses of people, trying to estimate the
numbers.

One hundred thousand, they thought at first, but as
more and more came on foot or by carriage, the estimate rose until it was certain there were more than
five hundred thousand people in Hyde Park that day.

Bugles from the van announced the beginning of the
speeches, but not everyone could get close enough to
hear. It didn't matter. On the fringes, deep inside the
lawns and trees of the park, impromptu boxes made
stands for impromptu speakers, and all could stroll from
one to the other and hear the messages.

Emmeline finished her own speech and then was free
to walk and mingle with the others. Harry was beside
her, looking so tall and handsome that she could not
believe Sylvia's warnings that the work in Glasgow was
too much for him and was undermining his health.
True, he was thin, but his fine features, so like her own,
were tanned and looked the better for his outdoor work.

She was too happy to worry. She wanted to reach out
and embrace every single one of these marvellous people
who had answered the W.S.P.U. call. She loved them—
the women in their summer dresses of white or coloured
muslins or lawns or cottons, their fringed parasols like

her own green one, their pretty ribbons and sashes.

A fair showing of men had come, too, she noticed. Some were escorting wives or daughters or mothers; some were politicians, anxious to be seen as supporting the cause; others had come on their own and were surrounded by pretty girls selling them rosettes or buttons or picture postcards.

Emmeline could not take a step without being greeted by someone or introduced to someone. "Is this your son? How much he looks like you," said a friend. "Isn't this a glorious day for us, Mrs. Pankhurst?" said another. "Mrs. Pankhurst, may I introduce my mother to you?" —"My father—" "My sister . . ." Over and over she heard: "Did you ever believe so many people would come? Isn't it wonderful?"

Mrs. Despard said it when they met. Though they had separated and Mrs. Despard was now head of the Women's Freedom League, they were both militant women and there was no bitterness between them, no ill feeling. Emmeline agreed with her that she had never thought so vast a crowd was possible. This was the greatest day of her life.

She couldn't possibly ever be any happier, she thought. But then she caught sight of Christabel up on the speaker's platform, and she made a secret reservation deep in her heart. The happiest day to come would be the day when Christabel Pankhurst would be elected the first woman member of Parliament. This was Emmeline's new hope and her most yearning dream.

The holiday spirit among the enormous crowd seemed to mount in spiralling waves of joy, as each speaker called for the final push to get the suffrage vote through Parliament. The name Asquith was on every speaker's lips and went echoing through the park. This was Herbert Asquith, the new Liberal Prime Minister, who had superseded Sir Henry Campbell-Bannerman. Asquith was denounced in Hyde Park that day, but he had made a promise and the suffragettes were determined to hold him to it.

He had said his Government had a "binding obligation" to reform male suffrage and give votes to more men, and he had promised that Reform Bill would be the opportunity for a motion for woman suffrage. He had broken that promise, but surely he could not turn his back on such a demonstration of five hundred thousand people?

Even while the late afternoon shadows gathered in Hyde Park and the joyful crowd began slowly to disperse for their homes, Christabel rushed to the office to write out the resolutions that had been passed that day, and send them to the home of the Prime Minister.

The next morning the leaders of the W.S.P.U. were gathered in Christabel's office in Clement's Inn, busy with the hundred and one small tasks of cleaning up after such a glorious day—counting the money collected, setting up a room for the lost-and-found objects brought from Hyde Park, holding informal conferences with branch W.S.P.U. leaders—when Mr. Asquith's reply was brought.

It was a short note. It brusquely referred Miss Pankhurst to his last statement on the matter, in which he had said woman suffrage was somewhere in "a remote and speculative future."

They looked at each other appalled. Though it was still a sunny day outside, the office suddenly seemed dark and cold and cheerless. They had been so certain of victory that this defeat seemed impossible to understand or bear.

"Five hundred thousand people—didn't it mean anything to the Prime Minister?" Mrs. Pethick-Lawrence asked. She sounded dazed.

"He's thinking of millions of male votes, the ones that put him in office," said her husband. "The woman vote is a potential, but the ones he's thinking of are actual. Our numbers seem large to us, but perhaps they seem small to him."

"Then," said Christabel, coming out of her shock, "we'll show him we are not just numbers. We're a force. *Force majeure* was what Mr. Gladstone said the Government would respect, and he was right. Women won't earn respect by having a great picnic in Hyde Park; they'll earn it with weapons in their hands!"

When the news spread of Asquith's reply, the membership of the W.S.P.U. and their sympathizers were as angry and mutinous as was Christabel. They flocked to a hastily called public meeting in Parliament Square on June 30. When the police prevented them from entering the square, the women climbed up on iron railings around it, sang and shouted defiance from Broad Sanctuary and many of them were arrested.

Frustrated at not being able to reach Parliament, two

women went to the Prime Minister's residence at No. 10
Downing Street and threw a stone through his window.
They were arrested, too, but for the first time the women
had taken a weapon in their hands; the first blow had
been struck.

Emmeline strongly defended the action at the next
At Home. "We would prefer to achieve our ends by
peaceful means, but if we cannot, we will throw stones.
Make no mistake. We are in a war where the Government has all the advantage, but as long as any woman
can pick up a stone and throw it, she is not defenceless.
She is not in retreat."

The summer of 1908 was extremely hot. Emmeline
knew what the suffragettes sent to Holloway must be
suffering in their unventilated cells. Even the *Manchester Guardian* newspaper wrote that "their stringent imprisonment . . . violates the public conscience."

The women pledged themselves to vengeance for the
prisoners. Parliament recessed for the summer, but politicians were holding meetings at home with their con-
stituents, and at every such meeting the women appeared
to heckle and harass. Special targets were Asquith and
Winston Churchill, but another was Lloyd George, the
Chancellor of the Exchequer.

Lloyd George became so enraged at the interruptions
during his speeches that he declared the women should
be gagged or have sacks put over their heads. He ordered his stewards to "ruthlessly throw the women out."

Except for the two women who had thrown the stone
at No. 10 Downing Street, all the prisoners were out of
gaol by the time Parliament convened on October 12.

The W.S.P.U. planned a giant demonstration for the following day. To inspire a large attendance at that Caxton Hall demonstration, with its march to Parliament, it was decided to first hold an invitation rally in Trafalgar Square on the 11th.

The wording of the call to the Caxton Hall meeting had given the planners in Clement's Inn a great deal of trouble.

"Men and Women," Mr. Pethick-Lawrence had written, "Help the Suffragettes to . . ." But then he was stuck. To do what? "Help make a protest?" he suggested.

"Help demand an audience?" Emmeline proposed, but none of them liked that wording. "We need a word that demonstrates action."

Christabel had the answer. "Why not put 'Help the Suffragettes to Rush the House of Commons, on Tuesday Evening, October 13, at 7:30?'" she suggested. And so it was decided. The word "rush" gave just the feeling of urgency and motion they wanted to express.

Leaflets which carried this call were printed in great numbers and distributed.

Just before Parliament convened, Emmeline had to settle a personal problem. She had not believed Sylvia when she said Harry's health was poor, but the Glasgow builder who employed Harry had written to her saying that he must not come back to Scotland. The boy could not stand another cold, rainy winter of outside work.

Perplexed as to what to do with him, Emmeline finally arranged for him to catch up with his schoolwork in the British Museum Library, working alone, and she would also pay for shorthand-typing classes. Out of her small salary she arranged lodgings for him in London, and allowed him a pound a week for expenses. Sylvia and Christabel—united for once—took him to an oculist and had him fitted with glasses.

Emmeline was having to admit to herself that her son, unlike her daughters, had no strong incentive to his life. When he was supposed to be studying at the library, she would find him at Clement's Inn, only happy when he was given some small task to do. But she had more pressing matters to think about.

Crowds began arriving early at Trafalgar Square on the afternoon of the 11th, milling about the base of the statue of Nelson or about the great stone lions. When Emmeline and Christabel and Flora Drummond walked out on the temporary platform below the statue, the square was packed with people.

Mrs. Drummond spoke well on the history of the suffragette movement. Emmeline reminded the crowd of the promises made and broken by the Government, and urged everyone to come to Caxton Hall or go to Parliament Square on the 13th, to support the W.S.P.U. delegation to the House of Commons.

Christabel repeated the invitation. "I wish you all to be there on the evening of the 13th, and I hope that will be the end of this movement," she said. "Years ago John Bright [who led demands for male suffrage] told the people that it was only by lining the streets from Charing Cross to Westminster that they could impress the Government. Well, we are only taking a leaf out of his book. We want you to help the women to rush their way into the House of Commons. . . . If you are afraid, we will take the lead and you will follow us."

As the meeting came to a close, Flora Drummond whispered to Emmeline: "I saw Lloyd George on the edge of the crowd. What do you suppose he was doing there?"

At noon the next day, October 12, the three women, Emmeline, Christabel and Mrs. Drummond, were served with warrants that read:

"Information has been laid this day by the Commissioner of Police for that you in the month of October in the year 1908 were guilty of conduct likely to provoke a breach of the peace by initiating and causing to be initiated, by publishing and causing to be published, a certain handbill, calling upon and inciting the public to do a certain wrongful and illegal act, viz., to rush the House of Commons at 7:30 p.m. on October 13th inst."

The warrant ended with a notice that the women were to appear at the Bow Street police station that afternoon at three o'clock.

Two things were obvious. The word "rush" in the leaflets had given the authorities their excuse for the warrants, and the order to appear so immediately in court was meant to frustrate the next evening's demonstration in front of Parliament.

Emmeline quickly sent off a note to the Bow Street magistrate. "It does not suit our convenience to obey the summons quite so early," she wrote. "We shall be in our headquarters, No. 4 Clement's Inn, at six o'clock tomorrow evening, and will then be entirely at your disposal."

The three then went to Queen's Hall, where an At
Home was being held of the most active W.S.P.U. members to make final plans for the October 13 demonstration. "No matter what happens to us, you must carry
on," Emmeline told them, and they promised they would.

At precisely six o'clock Mrs. Drummond drove up in
a cab to Clement's Inn and the Pankhursts walked down-
stairs to meet the police officers, who took them in custody and escorted them to the Bow Street station. It was
too late in the day for a court hearing; they were held
without bail and put into cells for the night.

Emmeline could not sleep for wondering what was
happening in Parliament Square, and the next morning
she saw the newspapers. The response to the leaflet call
had far exceeded her hopes—newspaper estimations went
from sixty thousand to one hundred thousand people
who had lined the streets, made a solid mass around
three sides of the square or joined in with the deputa-
tions of women marching from Caxton Hall with resolutions to hand in to the House of Commons. Six thousand
police had been called out to stop the suffragettes, and
they had arrested twenty-four women.

What particularly excited Emmeline was the report in
the newspapers that the immense crowd had been mainly
sympathetic. As the women had tried, over and over
again, to "rush" through the police cordons to reach
the entrance, people from the sidelines had called out:
"This way! Over here—we'll help you! We'll clear a
way for you!"

She doubted very much that all sixty or one hundred
thousand people in that crowd cared about woman suf-

frage, but perhaps they did care for fair play, and were indignant that the women should not have been peacefully allowed to hand in their resolutions to the House. Perhaps they had admired the stubborn courage of the suffragettes as they refused to be pushed back, and had run, dodging and twisting, through the police cordon to reach their goal.

The magistrate would claim, she knew, that this had been a riot. If so, who was to blame—the women, who were going about a lawful, peaceful errand, or the police, who had stopped them?

When Emmeline was taken from her cell to the courtroom that morning, she found it packed with people. The charge was read and then, as prearranged, Christabel rose to declare that she was acting not only as defendant but as lawyer for the three. There was consternation at this announcement. While it was true that Christabel had her degree and could put Ll.B. after her name, women were not supposed to practice before the bar.

Judge Curtis Bennet made his decision, bending over backwards to display his fairness to the defendants. He had no objection, he said, to Miss Pankhurst's defending herself and the other two, if that was what they wished.

He regretted his decision immediately. Christabel demanded a trial by jury. He refused that, but he had to agree to a week's adjournment of the trial to let her prepare her case. That morning he realized, with shock, that this young woman knew her law and her rights and was prepared to fight for them.

The trial began on October 21. First, the prosecution put on its witnesses. These were policemen, who swore

that the situation in front of Parliament Square had been
fraught with danger to life and limb. Others, in plain
clothes, had stood in Trafalgar Square on the 11th and
heard the defendants urge women to "rush" the House
of Commons, to attack and storm it.

Then it was the turn of the defence lawyer, Miss
Christabel Pankhurst. What was immediately clear was
that if women had been allowed to become barristers in
England, she would have gained fame as a brilliant coun-
sel. She was brainy and she was audacious.

She announced the witnesses she had subpoenaed.
Gasps went up in the courtroom. She was putting the
enemy on the stand to prove her own case! Her witnesses
were the Right Honourable David Lloyd George, Chancellor of the Exchequer, and the Right Honourable Herbert Gladstone, Home Secretary. She had many other witnesses to call, but these two Cabinet members, she hoped,
would convict the Government of hypocrisy out of their
own mouths.

They had not come of their own accord, but had
been subpoenaed. They were hostile and uncomfortable.
Lloyd George was first on the stand. Being a lawyer himself, he quickly saw through the cleverness of Christabel's
questions to him. She was trying to make him say what
he thought of the Trafalgar Square meeting, of the
danger at Parliament Square, of the whole suffrage cause.

He was trapped. As a member of the Cabinet, he had
to back the arrests of the Trafalgar Square speakers and
the police action at Parliament Square, yet as the questioning went on he found he could not do so. Miss Pankhurst was too smart for him. He could only evade when

the questions got too hot, and look to the judge to get
him out of trouble.

At first he claimed he had heard Mrs. Pankhurst ask
the audience at Trafalgar to force an entrance to the
House of Commons, but backed down and admitted she
had not said "force." He had to admit that the speeches
had not been inflammatory. He admitted that he had
taken his own little six-year-old daughter to Parliament
Square the night of the 13th to watch the happenings,
and there had been no danger for himself or his child
in the crowd.

She asked him his personal opinion of the leaflet and
if he thought it incited to violence. Lloyd George looked
to the judge, who hastily came to his rescue. The judge
would decide the meaning of the leaflet; she was not to
ask Mr. Lloyd George.

Christabel then asked him to define the word "rush."

"I cannot undertake to do that," he replied.

"You cannot offer any definition of the word "rush"?
Well, I will suggest some to you," she said. "I find that
in Chambers' English Dictionary one of the meanings is
an 'eager demand.' " When Lloyd George said he would
accept that, Christabel went on: "Now, if you were called
upon to help the suffragettes to make an eager demand
to the House of Commons that they should give votes
to women, would you feel we were calling upon you to
do an illegal act?"

If Lloyd George said no, he was on the side of the
suffragettes. If he said yes, he made himself ridiculous.
A buzz of comment went around the courtroom. Emmeline, sitting in the prisoners' dock, saw two newspaper-

men look at each other and then at Christabel, with
amazed admiration

Again the judge had to help Lloyd George out of his
dilemma, but Christabel went on with the same sort of
questions. Even if Judge Bennett had to save the witness,
Lloyd George's evasions and his refusals to answer were
a testimony in themselves.

Her last question was so adroitly made that again
Lloyd George was in a trap. She led up to it with other
questions about incitements to violence, then she asked
him what about his own public words at a public meeting when he had told his stewards to "ruthlessly throw
the women out." Was not that a real incitement to violence?

At this neat turning of the tables, the courtroom exploded into laughter. The judge pounded for silence.

Christabel Pankhurst, clad in her favourite green dress
and moving with her own peculiar light grace of a
dancer, was the dominant figure in the room. With a con-
temptuous gesture, she dismissed the Honourable Lloyd
George from the stand.

~//~ Chapter six

She called her next witness, Herbert Gladstone, the Home Secretary. Between the office of Home Secretary and the police department there was a direct link, and Christabel wanted to prove this. However, the judge stopped that line of questioning quickly—though not before she had made her point.

Frustrated, she turned to the witness' hypocrisy. The Home Secretary ordered out police to stop women, while this same Mr. Gladstone, candidate for Parliament, had once urged women on.

Had he not once said he was in favour of woman suffrage? "Yes," answered Mr. Gladstone.

"Did you say," asked Christabel, "that men had had to struggle for centuries for their political rights? Did you say there comes a time when political dynamics are far more important than political arguments?"

Again he had to respond, "Yes."

"And that men had learned that lesson? And that they know the necessity for demonstrating that *force majeure* . . . ?"

"Yes," he said.

"Then you cannot condemn our methods any more?" she flung at him.

Like Lloyd George, he was trapped. He could only mutter, "That is hardly a matter of my opinion," and look to the judge for help. Judge Bennett quickly ruled that the witness did not have to answer. But he had not been able to save Mr. Gladstone from revealing that his words and his actions made lies of each other.

After getting the Home Secretary to admit that the meaning of the word "rush" was to move speedily, not to assault, she let him go.

Her other witnesses—which included a member of Parliament, Mr. Murray; Colonel Percy Massey; Lady Constance Lytton; and a noted authoress, Miss Evelyn Sharp—all stated they had heard nothing inflammatory at the Trafalgar Square meeting, and there had been no danger to life or limb in Parliament Square. All declared it had been the action of the police, not the action of the women, that had led to the trouble.

The questioning and cross-examination were at last over. All that remained were the final statements of the defendants.

As a lawyer, Christabel had done brilliantly, but she had been hedged around and frustrated by the judge's rulings. He would not permit her to go into the *why* of either the leaflet or the demonstration. But it was customary for wide latitude to be given to the defendants' own closing statements; not even Judge Bennett dared censor them. Now the three women could say why they had done what they did.

Christabel spoke first. The right for a hearing of a

political petition, she said, was a right that stemmed from the Magna Carta and it applied to women as well as men —or should. The Government had refused to hear the petition and had ordered out the police because it feared the strength of the woman suffrage movement.

Out of that fear had come malice—malicious charges and arrests to try to silence the women's leaders.

Did not the W.S.P.U. have a right to "incite" women to present themselves at Parliament with a peaceful resolution? Did they not have the right to call upon all people to come and witness their attempt? Were these not open and honest dealings?

And she ended her speech by saying that the prisoners would not defend themselves by promising not to petition again. "I do not want you, sir," addressing Judge Bennett, "to suppose . . . I have wished to make any apology. Far from it. . . . If we go to prison, when we come out, we shall be ready to issue another bill calling upon the public to compel the House of Commons and compel the Government to do us justice."

She sat down. There was spontaneous applause, which the judge stopped with a severe reprimand. Then it was Emmeline's turn to speak for herself.

A silence fell over the whole courtroom as the mother took the daughter's place at the front of the dock. Emmeline Pankhurst was now fifty years old, and there was nothing youthful left in her thin face, with the violet shadows under her eyes and the curving hollows under her cheekbones. Her black hair was streaked with grey. The slender, erect figure was no longer supple; she held her shoulders with arrogance now, with imperiousness.

She had done herself honour not the court, by wearing her best costume of grey twill, with a high-boned collar sewn with tiny seed pearls.

So queenly was her appearance that even the judge inclined his head, in a half bow, as she stepped forward to speak.

Her first words challenged his right to preside over her. "We are not women," she said, "who would come into this court as ordinary lawbreakers, and we feel it is a great indignity. . . . We do not object to that if from that degradation we shall ultimately succeed in winning political reform for the women of this country."

She told them, briefly, of her childhood and its comforts, but also of the discrimination between the boys and girls of her family, and the education that had fitted her for nothing practical. Then she spoke of her marriage to a fine man, who had taught her that women were the equal of men, and of his death and how she had had to work to support her family. She recounted what she had learned in that job of man's inhumanity towards women, and of the terrible need women had for justice and protection under the law.

Was it any wonder that she had decided to devote her life to winning equality for women?

As she talked, it was noticeable that there were men in that courtroom who lowered their eyes and kept them down, so as not to look at her—and one of these was Judge Bennett himself.

"I have tried constitutional methods. I have been womanly," she said. Judge Bennett had once berated some other suffragette prisoners for being "unwomanly"

in their behaviour."We have tried to be womanly," she
repeated, "we have tried to use feminine influence, and
we have seen it is of no use. We are here today because
we are driven here. We have taken this action because, as
women, it is our duty even to break the law in order to
call attention to the reasons why we do so."

The silence in the room was absolute. The judge did
not move. The clerk held papers tight in his hands as if
he did not dare shuffle them. A young policeman was cry-
ing, but he did not even wipe the tears that trickled down
his face.

"If you decide against us, to prison we must go. . . .
We are driven to this; we are determined to go on with
the agitation; we are in honour bound to do so until we
win. We believe that if we get the vote it will mean
changed conditions for our less fortunate sisters. We are
not here because we are lawbreakers; we are here in our
efforts to become law*makers*."

She sat down to silence, which held until Flora Drummond got up to make her speech. Then throats were
cleared, papers rattled and held-in breaths let out in deep
sighs. Mrs. Drummond made a spirited defence of her
work and actions, and she won sympathy throughout the
court.

But none of the speeches were to any avail, officially.
The verdict had been settled long before. Judge Bennett
ruled that the handbill was a likely instrument to create
breaches of the peace. He sentenced the two older
women, Mrs. Pankhurst and Mrs. Drummond, to three
months' imprisonment, and Christabel to ten weeks.

Once again Emmeline rode in the prison van to Holloway Gaol. But no sooner were the three women inside than Emmeline demanded of the wardresses that they send immediately for the prison Governor. She overawed them and they brought him.

"Sir," she said, "suffragettes are committed to this second division of Holloway by gross injustice." The second was for ordinary criminals; the first division, with better treatment, for political prisoners. "Therefore, we will not submit to being treated as criminals. We insist upon dressing privately; we insist upon communication, which means adjoining cells for us. We will not observe the rule of silence during exercise periods. I know that the injustice to us is not your fault, but we must insist upon our rights."

They weren't "rights" at all, but the Governor gave in on the first two points. He was accustomed to dealing firmly with the prostitutes and thieves who came his way, but he was not used to someone as autocratic as Mrs. Pankhurst. The suffragettes were allowed some measure of privacy and were placed in cells next to each other, where they could hear each other speak and cheer each other up.

But he said that the rule of silence during exercise was not to be broken—and Emmeline resolved to break it.

When she was taken out into the dismal courtyard of the prison, where the women shuffled around in single file under the watchful eyes of the wardresses, she spied Christabel and called to her: "Stand still, Christabel, until I reach you and we can talk."

Instantly a wardress rushed up to her to stop her, while another went for help. Emmeline paid no attention; she walked on until she reached Christabel, linked her hand in her daughter's arm and whispered quietly to her. "Did you know they have released Flora Drummond because of her health?"

Just then more wardresses came rushing into the yard. They grabbed Emmeline and hurried her back inside, followed by Christabel, but not before the other prisoners had raised a cheer for the Pankhursts.

For defiance, Christabel got three days of solitary confinement. Emmeline, as the instigator of the mutiny, was classed as a "dangerous criminal" and was given a week in a damp, dark cell and was refused all exercise or communication with anyone. Her cell door was solid, with only an opening for food to be pushed through, and that door cut off all sight and sound.

For one of her temperament, solitary confinement was the cruellest of punishments. She suffered terribly. All day long she sat on the plank bed or paced the small stone floor, yearning for a whisper of a voice or even a glimpse of the wardress' face through the slot in the door. The inaction and the empty, dark silence tore at her nerves. But she survived.

By the end of that ordeal she knew she could stand anything that might come to her, and she also knew she would go on and repeat her offence. Any punishment was better than submitting like a dumb animal to fate. She was Emmeline Pankhurst, and she would let no one forget it.

She found out, when she returned to her other cell next to Christabel's, that the world outside had not forgotten her. They could whisper to each other through

the bars, and Christabel told her the news that had fil-
tered into the gaol.

The suffragettes outside were showing their indigna-
tion over the trial and the sentences by militant protests.
The W.S.P.U. was staging daily demonstrations at the
gates of Holloway; great protest meetings were held
throughout all of Britain. But the most dramatic protest
was made by the Women's Freedom League, the militant
organization founded by Mrs. Despard when she left the
W.S.P.U.

Mrs. Despard and a Miss Muriel Matters had procured
seats in the Ladies' Gallery of the House of Commons,
and then quietly, under cover of their cloaks, chained
and padlocked their wrists to the iron grille. Through
that grille they called out to the House below: "What
are you going to do about votes for women? When are
you going to release Mrs. Pankhurst?"

Attendants rushed to evict them—and couldn't. It took
a long time to get a locksmith and have him saw through
the chains, and in the meantime the House was in consternation as the two ladies chanted their questions over
and over. For once women had a voice in the House,
even if they had to handcuff themselves to get it!

The Prime Minister and the Cabinet were besieged in
their offices and homes, and could rarely escape for any
pleasant hours of social life. As likely as not, Mr. Asquith
would find himself at a social function talking to a
beautifully gowned and titled lady, when she would suddenly grab him by the lapels of his coat and demand:
"When are you going to release Mrs. Pankhurst? When
are you going to give suffrage to women?"

At a meeting where Lloyd George spoke, the front rows were occupied by women who, at a given signal, stood up and threw open their coats. Underneath they were wearing copies of Holloway prison uniforms and they shouted in unison: "Votes for Women, *Now!*"

The pavements of London and all principal cities were scrawled with suffragette messages; the newspaper *Votes for Women* redoubled its circulation. Posters were pasted up on prominent city buildings in the dark of night. One of the cleverest of these was of two series of drawings. The top series said "Men can be this" and pictured a drunkard, a gambler and so on—"yet they can vote"; the bottom strip pictured women as mothers, as teachers, as nurses and said: "yet they cannot vote."

Mr. Pethick-Lawrence, in an editorial in *Votes for Women,* made an interesting point. He showed that women, by their very struggle for the vote, were coming out of their shells and proving they had the qualities of organization, of leadership, of bold and creative imagination, which were the very qualities men said they did not possess and so should not be in politics.

The women's actions must have had some effect. With no explanation offered, Emmeline and Christabel were released before their sentences were fully served. As the prison gates closed behind them, they were greeted by an astonishing sight. The streets around them were swept by a wave of women, all dressed in the W.S.P.U. colours of green, white and purple. In their centre was a carriage emblazoned with victory signs on it, and the horses' reins were held by proud young girls.

Between tears and laughter, Emmeline and Christabel

were helped into the carriage and the procession of
women followed, escorting them through the London
streets.

And at the Queen's Hall that night there was a grand
formal reception. Girls in white dresses, trimmed in
purple and green, went through a marching ceremony,
carrying the banners and flags of the W.S.P.U. up to the
platform. Christabel was given a silk standard upon
which the dates of her imprisonment were inscribed,
while Emmeline received a beautiful necklace of semi-
precious stones in the Union colours.

Most of this had been Mrs. Pethick-Lawrence's doing,
and Emmeline found that that capable woman, with the
assistance of Mrs. Drummond, Sylvia, Annie Kenney and
a good office staff, was energetically carrying forward the
work of the W.S.P.U. There was work there for Emmeline, but no worries.

Her real worry was a personal one. She simply did not
know what to do about Harry. With Emmeline and his
eldest sister on trial and then in prison, he had found it
impossible to spend his days quietly studying or learning
shorthand. He had neglected that, and devoted himself
to running errands for everyone at Clement's Inn. It was
his way of serving his mother's cause.

Sylvia had talked it over with him. His help was ap-
preciated, but the family would rather he would dis-
cover his own place in life and stand on his own feet. If
his studies bored him, what would he like to do instead?

Harry had thought he might like to become a farmer,
so arrangements were made for him to take a post as gar-
dener at a sanatorium. Within a very brief while, the

woman in charge of the sanatorium sent him back to London. He had a serious inflammation of the bladder, and when Emmeline came out of Holloway she found him recovering from it in the London nursing home run by nurses Catherine Pine and Townsend.

Those two women, devoted to the cause of woman suffrage, gave generously and freely of their professional talents. Their private rest home became an emergency hospital for the casualties of the warfare, and there was seldom a time when one or more women were not recovering there from the effects of prison life.

In this nursing home Emmeline found Harry, and she and Sylvia talked with him about his future. The idea of farming or gardening, a life on the land, appealed to the mother. It was the only thing Harry seemed ever to express a liking for, so she felt that was what he should do. She arranged that, as soon as he recovered, he would go to a place called Mayland in Essex, where he was to be a labourer and a student-farmer on the estate of a wealthy friend.

Sylvia protested. Though she had agreed to it before, she now thought Harry was just drifting into it for want of anything better, and that he was physically unfit to do outdoor work in all kinds of weather.

Her mother would not listen to her. As soon as Harry was over the bladder infection, he was sent off to Mayland. To Emmeline's eyes he looked the picture of health.

It was Harry's misfortune to be born into a family of dynamic women. He never matured. What his mother and sisters thought and did and suffered for was of such great consequence that his own personality never devel-

oped. Just as his outwardly strong body concealed a
physical weakness, his sweetness hid a nature that was
passive, that never acted for itself but was acted upon by
others. The main thought of his life was to please his
mother.

To her credit, this is not what she demanded or wanted
of him. She would have been happier if he had gone his
way and found his own fulfillment. She was glad he sym-
pathized with woman suffrage, but he had no talents for
leadership, and she wanted some other purpose in his life
than chalking suffragette notices on pavements.

Sylvia understood Harry, because she had struggled
with the same problem. Emmeline Pankhurst was too
important in their lives. They might criticize her, be
hurt by her or resent her, but they were utterly devoted
to her. She made every other person seem lifeless by com-
parison, and any other interest seemed paltry compared
to hers.

The artist in Sylvia had given way to the crusader, because in that way she could be more like Emmeline. How
could Harry concentrate on shorthand or a library or
even a farm when the centre of all excitement revolved
around his mother's work?

Unlike Harry, though, Sylvia had found in herself a
capacity to *be* a crusading leader, and she enjoyed it. She
was no longer torn with regrets for her art. Also, she had
had, in her father and in Keir Hardie, two other idols to
balance her devotion. She took her ideals from them,
too. Harry had only his mother to worship, without the
strength to match hers, without any gifts of his own.

As the year 1908 drew to a close, neither Emmeline

nor Sylvia had much time to worry about Harry. Thousands of women all over Britain were becoming militant suffragettes, forming W.S.P.U. chapters and looking to Clement's Inn for directions. Emmeline was in and out of London, speaking and organizing, swept along on a tide of activity that gave her no rest.

On January 25, 1909, four women were arrested for merely knocking at the Prime Minister's residence and asking to see Mr. Asquith. A month later a deputation, led by Mrs. Pethick-Lawrence, Lady Constance Lytton and Miss Daisy Solomon, went to the House of Commons with a resolution, and they were arrested and sent to Holloway for two weeks.

Emmeline was furious. The Government was treating the suffragettes with contempt, merely brushing them off its official doorsteps and sweeping them into gaol.

She convened another Parliament on February 29. "The Government," she told the hundreds of faithful members in Caxton Hall, "is behaving outrageously. Tonight we shall test, once and for all, if Mr. Asquith is willing to break the sacred laws he has sworn to uphold. We shall go to Parliament, following the best legal advice on how to proceed."

All the women present were to walk to the House of Commons in relays of twelve at a time, she explained, thus keeping within the strict letter of the law under the Charles II Act. Each group was to walk single file down the streets. They were to obey police orders. If the police tried to stop them presenting their petitions, however, they were to disregard them and consider the police actions illegal.

This night's action had been widely publicized. At the very moment Emmeline was addressing Caxton Hall, Keir Hardie was on his feet in the House of Commons, demanding that the delegations from the women be received and that orderly arrangements be made for their reception and hearing.

Mr. Gladstone, the Home Secretary answered: "I cannot say what action the police should take in this matter."

Hardie jumped up again, and so did other woman suffrage supporters, asking what the Home Secretary meant by that. The police? If the delegations were peacefully received, there would be no need of police. And if the Home Secretary claimed not to know what the police intended to do, he was a liar.

While the uproar was going on in the House, the first twelve women were approaching the House of Parliament, led by Emmeline Pankhurst, Mrs. Paul Solomon (Daisy), whose husband had been a colonial Prime Minister, and Miss Neligan, a prominent woman educator. It was seven thirty in the evening, crisp and cool, and the street-corner gas lamps burned steadily over their heads, with enough light to show the pavements densely jammed with onlookers.

There were so many that Emmeline was forced to lead her group down the middle of the street. She was glad there was no wind. She hated parading past watchers when she had to hang on to her hat and skirts. Tonight was calm, but frosty, and she warmed her hands in her muff, taking care not to crumple the petition she carried.

Policemen were stationed along the way. They said

nothing to her. They held the crowds back, turning their heads, warily, only when someone shouted: "We're with you, Mrs. Pankhurst!" or—much less often—"Go home where you belong!"

A block behind her, the second group of twelve was keeping its distance from hers; the third relay was near Scotland Yard, and the fourth was just rounding the turn at Trafalgar Square to begin the straight march to Parliament. Just ahead of Emmeline rode a W.S.P.U. woman on horseback. Her appearance was the typical dramatic Pankhurst touch—a young herald going slow-paced before, to announce to Parliament that its subjects were approaching.

Emmeline's group reached Parliament Square to find it empty, as the police held back the pressing throng of people. Directly in front of the Stranger's Entrance a solid mass of police blocked her way, but as she and Mrs. Solomon approached them they parted to make a lane for her.

Her heart bounded. The Government must have yielded. They must have decided to let the delegations into the House to speak their piece and be heard.

But at the entrance she was met by an inspector, who handed her a note. She read it aloud. It stated: "The Prime Minister, for the reasons which he has already given in a written reply to their request, regrets that he is unable to receive the proposed deputation."

She dropped the note on to the ground. She said, in a clear and ringing voice: "I stand upon my rights, as a subject of the King, to petition the Prime Minister, and I am firmly resolved to stand here until I am received."

Policemen seized her arms. Inspector Jarvis ordered her to leave. Ordinarily she would have struggled with them and tried to force her way past them, but tonight she was burdened with another responsibility. Both Mrs. Solomon and Miss Neligan were elderly ladies, and she did not want them hurt. To register her protest, she did what Christabel had once done—made a technical assault. She struck Inspector Jarvis lightly on the cheek. He understood. He put them under arrest.

The second and third delegations had arrived. The police blocked their way. They tried to get past and, as more and more women came into the square, more and more were arrested. The night's haul into police vans was a large one.

It was made even larger when the women coming behind learned what had happened and they had been refused a hearing. Their tempers boiled over. They roamed all night through the area of government buildings, throwing stones and smashing windows at the Admiralty office, the Home Office, the Treasury and Privy Council offices.

One hundred and eight women were arrested that night.

The fourteen women who were caught smashing windows went to gaol immediately, but the W.S.P.U. could make a political, test trial of the others. Emmeline was chosen to be the defendant for all of them. Her barrister, Lord Cecil, made such a good defence, and the magistrate, Sir Albert de Rutzen, was so perplexed in his mind as to why the women were not allowed to present peaceful petitions that, although he passed sentence on the more than a hundred women, he also suspended the sentences. Let a higher court rule on the political and legal points, not him!

The fourteen in gaol took a hint from Emmeline's mutiny during her imprisonment and defied all authority. To emphasize their protests, they went on a hunger strike.

Emmeline was both admiring of their courage and appalled at what these women, young and old, were doing to themselves. How could their bodies survive without food?

That the hunger strike was a most effective weapon in the struggle soon became evident. The newspapers made much of it, and many newspaper stories were sympathetic. Breaking windows was a shocking thing, certainly, but had not the women been driven to it, just as they were now driven to the heroism of the hunger strike? Was the Government to find itself responsible for their deaths?

Evidently not. Word was quietly passed to the prison officials, and the women were released before they could injure themselves seriously.

As soon as the fourteen had somewhat recovered their health, they came to Queen's Hall and told their experiences. That of Lucy Barnes, a young W.S.P.U. member, was typical. She told of how the fourteen prisoners had linked arms and stood against the wall to resist the order to strip and put on prison uniforms. The Governor had been called. He blew his whistle, and a large group of hefty wardresses had flown at the prisoners, forcing the girls apart and dragging them off to cells. Lucy, fighting hard, was surrounded by twelve wardresses, who tripped her and threw her to the ground and dragged her along by her hair. In her cell her clothing was ripped off and the uniform put on her, and she was tossed on to the bed.

When she refused to eat she was threatened, bullied and finally coaxed. Tempting hot dishes were brought to her cell and left there, but she resisted. The first day had not been so bad, nor the second, but by the third she was in pain and by the fourth she was weak and feverish.

Listening, Emmeline thought to herself that she had more than three daughters. All these brave, wonderful girls seemed as dear to her as her own children. She had to do for them what she had done for Christabel and Sylvia and Adela—be strong enough to let them make their own sacrifices. In the undemocratic W.S.P.U. one word from Emmeline would have stopped all hunger strikes. She did not give that word. Instead she vowed that the next time she was in prison she would refuse to eat, too.

The Pankhursts were heroines to the suffrage movement, but they were by no means the only ones. Hundreds of women, their names forgotten in history, went to gaol over and over and suffered what the Pankhursts did, but without enjoying their fame. Individual women showed individual bravery far beyond what was expected of them.

Such a woman was Lady Constance Lytton, a delicate woman in her forties, with a serious heart disease. On her first arrests she found she was treated with exceptional consideration and singled out from among the other prisoners for special courtesies. Was this because of her heart or her title? She wondered about it.

So in January of 1910 a "Jane Walton," a seamstress, was arrested for suffragette activity in Liverpool, and got fourteen days at hard labour. She went on a hunger strike and was forcibly fed by means of a rubber tube pushed down her throat, a terribly painful process. She refused to do the hard labour required in her sentence and was punished for it.

A photograph of "Jane Walton" was published in the newspapers and recognized as that of Lady Constance Lytton. Prison authorities hastily released her, for which she was less than grateful. She denounced the authorities for giving one kind of prison treatment to the poor and unknown and favoured treatment to the rich and titled.

The true heroines of the suffrage movement were the poor working girls who went to gaol over and over again, who received the harshest treatment and whose sacrifices went unnoticed by the newspapers.

~//~ Chapter seven

Late in the winter of 1909, Harry Pankhurst was stricken with polio and was brought to the Pine and Townsend nursing home in London, where he lay paralysed from the waist down. For weeks Emmeline did not leave the nursing home, and rarely was she away from Harry's bedside.

In the intervals when doctors and nurses banished her from his room she clung to Sylvia. Self-reproach was mingled with her grief. Was she responsible for this? She should have looked after Harry better; she should have listened to Sylvia when she said farm life was too much for him. Had she neglected Harry?

Sylvia comforted her. The girl also insisted that her mother must go ahead with her commitment to the American suffrage organizations. They had invited Emmeline to come to the United States and tell them the truth of what was happening in Britain, and perhaps help to stir more militancy in America. The lecture tour was all arranged. It would be wrong to cancel it. There was nothing Emmeline could do for Harry that doctors and nurses could not do better.

Besides, the Americans were offering large fees for Emmeline's lectures, and she would need that money for
Harry's medical expenses and to pay for his care if he
was permanently disabled.

In actual fact, Sylvia thought Harry would be better
off without his mother hovering over him. Her anguish
hurt him too much.

The doctors assured the mother that Harry was im-
proving, so, though she sailed for America with a heavy
heart late in 1909, by the time she reached New York
Harbour her naturally optimistic temperament had re-
asserted itself. Harry was certain to get better, and she
would be returning to him with enough money to pro-
vide him with the best of care.

She was used to being recognized, applauded or hissed
in public, but she was unprepared for the furore of her
reception when the ship docked in New York. She found
herself a notorious person, besieged by newspapermen
and photographers and surrounded everywhere she went
by the sympathetic, the curious or the hostile. For a few
days she led a bewildered existence, giving interviews
and holding newspaper conferences which had been arranged by her American sponsors.

It seemed to her that, on the one hand, she was admired too much and, on the other, treated as a dangerous
visitor who should not have been allowed in America.
One prominent newspaper described her and her suffragettes as "hooligans."

Then came the night of her first speech at Carnegie
Hall. Every seat was sold. Backstage, Emmeline got a
glimpse of that sea of faces, with every gallery and bal-

cony filled, and wondered how she could make an impression on them and how she could get her message across to people who were such strangers to her. She had invested a little of the money from the tour in some simple but truly beautiful gowns, and she knew she looked well.

Then the chairman escorted her to her place on the platform, the curtains went up, there was a polite smatter of applause and she was introduced. Holding her speech in her hand, she stepped forward into the spotlight.

Suddenly she had an inspiration. Disregarding the original opening of her speech, she said in her cultured and ladylike voice:

"I am what you call a hooligan . . ."

She could get no further for a while. Carnegie Hall erupted in wild applause and uproarious laughter. Emmeline had won her audience. The contrast between that word and herself standing there so regal, so obviously a gentlewoman, was hilarious. It was the sort of joke that Americans particularly liked, and for the rest of her speech their mood swung to hers.

Votes for women was a cause with a long tradition of struggle in America, but at that moment in history the women of Britain were the more militant, and the story Emmeline unfolded for them was of great interest. It was the same everywhere she spoke, from New York to Boston, to Baltimore and on to Canada. The tour was a whirlwind success.

She was back in London just before Christmas. The news that met her was devastating. The doctors had to tell her that Harry would never walk again.

"It would be better if he was dead!" Emmeline cried out to Sylvia, who was not shocked. Emmeline did not really mean it for Harry. It was only that, for herself, the thought of lying paralysed for a lifetime would truly be worse than death.

But those words came back to haunt her. She was constantly at his bedside, and she was there when Harry took a turn for the worse. The old inflammation of his bladder, which he had had before, started up again. Doctors were hurriedly called. They shook their heads. There was little hope of recovery.

Christmas passed without Emmeline's knowing it. Adela was hastily summoned, and she and Christabel were at the hospital every day. But it was Sylvia who sat most often on the other side of Harry's bed, and who tried to divert her mother's agonized thought. She told Emmeline that Harry had confided in her that he had fallen in love with a girl and had, shyly, shown her the poetry he had written.

Emmeline only looked at Sylvia, bewildered and a little hurt. Harry could not be in love. He was just a boy. He belonged to his family, not to some unknown girl. And Sylvia, regarding her mother with new eyes, suddenly thought she had grown very, very old. Her shoulders were stooped. The black hair had a lot of grey in it.

Shortly after New Year and the coming of 1910, Harry Pankhurst died at the age of twenty. Emmeline was shattered by grief. She let Sylvia take charge, and the girl selected the inscription "Blessed are the pure in heart" for the gravestone. Only a few old friends, such as Keir Hardie, were asked to the funeral with the family.

"Blessed are the pure in heart." It was apt, they thought, as they looked at the grave. In his short life Harry had been all goodness and tender kindness, wanting only to be the perfect knight to his mother and sisters. His death was a blow to them all. Next to Christabel, Harry had been Emmeline's favourite child, and her sorrow was to become a constant sadness in her heart.

But life must go on. She turned, gratefully, to the challenge of work.

A general election was held early in 1910, to test whether the people wanted the Liberals to continue in power. The W.S.P.U. threw itself into the task of defeating Liberal candidates, as they would have done with any party in power which refused votes to women.

It was a tempestuous time. In front of every Liberal election meeting the women hung up a large, gruesome poster showing a defenceless woman prisoner held down while doctors and wardresses forced liquid food into her mouth by means of a thick tube. Forced-feeding shocked everyone. Doctors were protesting that it was cruel and dangerous.

The Liberal Party came back to Parliament as the leading group. They still held the Cabinet and the authority of government, but many of their men had been defeated and their numbers had dwindled. Word was brought to Emmeline that the Liberal leadership had learned its lesson and would like to see a woman suffrage bill introduced—but without any appearance that the women were forcing them to it.

Promptly she declared a truce. The W.S.P.U. would be quiet and wait to see what would happen. In June of

1910 King Edward VII died and was succeeded by King George V. It might mean that the new reign would usher in a new age, and votes for women would be a part of it. Women were eager to compromise, and anxious not to do anything which might embarrass their friends in Parliament.

Everything seemed hopeful. A non-party committee on woman suffrage was set up in the House of Commons, called the Conciliation Committee, headed by the Earl of Lytton as chairman. On it were twenty-five Liberals, seventeen Conservatives, six Irish Nationalists and six from the Labour Party. They drew up a Conciliation Bill.

The original bill, drafted by Dr. Pankhurst years before had given women suffrage on equal terms with men. This was not true of the new one. The Conciliation Bill proposed to give the vote only to women householders and to women occupiers of business premises paying ten pounds rental a year or more.

Keir Hardie and Sylvia and Adela argued against accepting it. It did not include the poor or working women. But Christabel, Emmeline, the other leaders of the W.S.P.U. and the heads of other suffragette organizations were for it. It was a beginning, they felt. Extension of suffrage to all women would come later.

Emmeline would listen to no arguments against it. She was eager for success, even if a partial one. Her enemies often said of her that she enjoyed being a martyr and loved the furore of arrests and the notoriety of trials. This was not true. She wanted to be the leader of a triumphant cause, not a lost one.

The bill was debated once, then came up for a second reading on July 11 and 12 and passed the House of Commons by the huge majority of 299 to 189.

In Clement's Inn that night of July 12 there was jubilation. For weeks the celebrations went on and on, with women gathering at meetings and tea parties to rejoice. At long last the dream had come true. Some women of Britain would go to the polls at the next election and cast their ballots along with men!

The joy was short-lived. In November, Prime Minister Asquith vetoed the bill on the flimsy ground that, as it was written, it could not be amended. He also declared that a re-written bill would have to wait until the next year for a hearing.

Immediately there was an uproar. While Keir Hardie and others were fiercely arguing the matter inside the House, the W.S.P.U. called an emergency meeting in Caxton Hall, and Emmeline announced, in a passion of anger: "The truce is over! We have been betrayed. Mr. Asquith must hear from us, with the largest delegations and the largest crowds he has ever seen!"

The date was set: November 18. Again they would hold their own Women's Parliament in Caxton Hall, and march from there in delegations of twelve. The first group, led by Emmeline, had been carefully chosen. It included Dr. Elizabeth Garrett Anderson, a pioneer woman doctor; Hertha Ayrton, a famous scientist; Mrs. Cobden-Sanderson; Princess Dhuleep Singh, of Indian royalty; Miss Neligan; Mrs. Solomon; a Mrs. Brackenbury, and four others.

As Emmeline walked out of Caxton Hall followed by

these women, to the cheers of the audience, no one would have recognized in her the broken and grieving mother of the previous January. Her shoulders were straight again; elasticity was back in her step; her eyes were flashing fire.

She carried her banner, reading "Asquith has vetoed our bill" down the streets in that late twilight of the November day, between long lines of cheering people. It was just after seven o'clock. The crowds must have hurried through their dinners; some had been standing and waiting a long time.

Enormous numbers of policemen were positioned in Parliament Square. They blocked her path, but people poured in from every side to help her, and it was they who struggled with the police to force a passageway for her group. Emmeline was glad of this. She would have pushed her way through, but three of her delegation were elderly women. They made it to the Stranger's Entrance and mounted the steps to shouts of triumph from the crowds.

Emmeline was about to go in; she was arguing with attendants. Suddenly she heard a scream behind her. She turned and beheld a scene of ghastly brutality.

The second and third delegations had reached Parliament Square, and the rest of the 450 women marchers were not far behind. Up until this terrible Friday in November the police had been rough, but not unduly so. They had made their arrests as swiftly as possible. This time their orders had been not to arrest, but to attack.

For a moment it seemed to Emmeline that all she could see were dark, swirling figures and all she could

hear were angry roars from the crowd and screams of
pain from the women marchers. Then her vision cleared
and she could see individuals.

Policemen had fallen upon the women with fists and
boots and clubs. Here they were dragging one by her
hair; there they were punching another. To the left,
Emmeline saw a woman knocked to the ground, get up
and stagger forward, only to be knocked down again.
Some of the police invented a game. They grabbed a
woman and threw her to another policeman, who tossed
her to another, thumping and hitting her as she was flung
around the square.

Women were lying on the stones and moaning. Men
and women from the watching crowd ran out to help,
and got the same treatment from the police. With each
passing moment more and more of the marching women
were arriving, and with each passing moment the fury of
the police mounted. Only a few swung their nightsticks,
but they were all using their fists and some even kicked
the fallen women on the ground.

Keir Hardie and other friends of the suffragettes had
come out of the House Chamber, taken one glimpse of
what was going on and raced back inside to demand the
Government stop the brutality going on outside. Emmeline tried to go down the steps to help, but she could
not get through the solid block of uniformed men below.
She retreated, helplessly, to the upper steps and watched
in growing horror.

The women would not be defeated. No matter what,
they were determined to carry out their task of bringing

their resolutions to the House. Although many were too hurt to move and had to be carried away, those who could still get back to their feet did their best to get past the police. And again and again the police advanced on them and struck and hit and pummelled and kicked them, until the darkening night was hideous with screams and cries of the women and the shocked murmurings of the huge crowd massed on the outskirts.

For five hours the one-sided battle raged. It was four hundred and fifty unarmed women against thousands of trained and burly policemen, but the women had courage on their side. They would not let themselves be turned back by force. With their clothing torn and their hair hanging dishevelled down their backs, they pushed and struggled their bruised bodies past one policeman and another, only to be struck down by the third.

No one tried to stop Emmeline from entering the lobby. Attendants, even police stationed there, fell back from the anguish and fury in her face. But when she demanded entrance into the House, they refused. Members of Parliament dashed in and out, running to see for themselves what was happening, running back and shouting for the Prime Minister.

But Mr. Asquith had discreetly disappeared.

"Is there not a man in the House of Commons who will stand up for us?" Emmeline cried out. "Is there not one who will stop this?"

This was unfair. There were men there as outraged and shocked as she was. Hardie was on his feet in the Chamber and making the angriest speech of his life, de-

manding that the police be ordered to stop. Lord Castle-
reigh looked out of the Strangers' Entrance and then talked
back inside the chamber to move that the Conciliation
Bill be put on the agenda immediately. But without the
Prime Minister this could not be done, and the Prime
Minister was gone.

Back and forth Emmeline and her small delegation
went between the closed doors of the House and the outside steps. Night had fallen. The police had pressed back
the crowd; mounted police manouvered their horses to
force people into side streets. Still the battle raged in the
square.

It was littered with torn banners, trampled to the
ground. There were fewer women now, as the badly injured were carried off, but those who remained resisted
all the more fiercely, and were more brutally handled.
Women were punched in the face, struck on the head,
bludgeoned and beaten and kicked. Suddenly Emmeline
saw a little figure being helped up the steps and saw that
it was frail and elderly Mrs. Solomon, her face disfigured
by a bruised cheek and a black eye. Somehow, in the very
beginning, she had become separated from the first delegation. In all the turmoil Emmeline had not noticed she
was missing.

Then the police vans, drawn by speeding horses, came
down into the square and it was all over. As fast as they
could the police rounded up and arrested the remaining
women, and shoved them into the vans. One hundred
and fifteen women and two men were arrested in all.

Slowly Emmeline, accompanied by her little group,

walked through the deserted square. In the House of
Commons the angry words were still flying about, but she
was too numb to care. The day, which would go down in
suffragette history as Black Friday, was over.

None of her own daughters had been involved in that
night's affair; they had been ordered to stay away, since
the W.S.P.U. had been certain that Emmeline would go
to gaol, and one leader in Holloway was enough at one
time. But her sister, Mary Clarke, had been one of the
women in the delegations and Emmeline was sick at the
thought of the gentle Mary, who was not strong, being
struck and beaten.

She heard footsteps behind her. Keir Hardie, his neck-
tie askew, his beard and hair wildly tangled as if he had
been ripping his hands through them, came up to take
her arm. "My God," he said, "but I will hold Winston
Churchill personally responsible for this. He's behind it,
and he'll answer for it tomorrow!"

Emmeline disengaged her arm from his hand. She was
enraged at all men. Even Hardie, old a friend as he was,
was a man, and she could hardly bear to look at him or
listen to him. She wasn't even grateful when he hailed
cabs and put her and her delegation into them. They
went to Caxton Hall.

It had been turned into a hospital, and volunteer doctors and nurses were working over the injured. It seemed
to her that everywhere she looked there were bruised,
swollen faces, cut lips and bleeding noses; doctors were
taping sprained angles and wrists and fingers. These were
the slightly hurt. The more seriously injured were lying

on stretchers, awaiting transfer to the Pine-Townsend Nursing Home or to hospitals, and on one stretcher Emmeline found her sister.

Mary Clarke had no obvious injury, but her colour and breathing were bad. The doctor whispered to Emmeline that he was afraid her heart had been seriously damaged by the brutal handling she had received. She had been repeatedly struck and knocked to the ground.

Some women were sobbing, but it was from pain or from nervous reaction, not from fear. Bloody Friday had not cowed their spirits. It had enraged them and strengthened their determination. Sylvia and Christabel were there, moving from woman to woman to get their stories for the records, and when Mary Clarke was taken away, Emmeline joined her daughters.

Everywhere she heard: "This is really war, Mrs. Pankhurst! We must fight back!" And when she embraced one weeping girl, the girl could only reproach herself. "I shouldn't have left just because I was hurt," she said. "I should have been arrested, too."

The next day, the charges against all the arrested women were abruptly dropped and they were freed. Even this, Keir Hardie charged in Parliament, was no act of mercy. Many of the newspapers had published outraged editorials and stories against the "Cossack" police. The Government was only trying to forestall further criticism, not admit its terrible mistake.

The Prime Minister and Cabinet, of course, denied any responsibility for Bloody Friday, but that was not believed. Hardie and the Conciliation Committee demanded an inquiry into the responsibility of Winston

Churchill, who was now Home Secretary. The investigation was denied. The committee then instituted its own
investigation and proved to its own satisfaction that the
police orders had indeed come from the Home Office.

Emmeline Pankhurst led hundreds of women to Downing Street, where they besieged the residence of the
Prime Minister. Windows were broken, and again Emmeline and one hundred and fifty-eight women were arrested, and again the charges were dropped.

The Americans were begging her to make another tour
of their country. Suffragette militancy was stirring there.
It was felt that Emmeline could do a lot to help her sisters in the United States and it was decided that she
should go. This time she had the story of Bloody Friday
to tell, and it sent a shock throughout all America. The
history of American suffrage had been as long as Britain's,
and there had been a few cases of brutality, but nothing
like this.

She came home. Again, she came home to a death. Her
sister, Mary Clarke, never fully recovered from the effects
of the beating she had undergone, and she died shortly
after Emmeline's return.

She was the first martyr of Bloody Friday. A Miss Hen-
riette William's heart had also become overstrained, and
she died on January 2, 1911; many others were to suffer
ill health the rest of their lives. But, while Mary Clarke's
loss was felt keenly by the Pankhurst family, they also
knew that since her marriage she had known nothing but
drab poverty and the heavy hand of an ill-tempered husband, and the one great experience of her life had been
the cause she died for.

When the King's Speech was read to the new session of Parliament in February of 1911, it made no mention of woman suffrage, but the Conciliation Committee was busy. It drew up a bill which it felt could not be vetoed again on purely technical grounds. Sir George Kemp and fifty members of the House demanded May 5 as the day for debate on the bill. Against all the Prime Minister's manoeuvres, they did secure that date.

The W.S.P.U. reluctantly agreed to a kind of truce. They would hold down, as much as possible, the militant defiance of suffragettes who wanted to hurl rocks at their enemies. Neither Emmeline nor Christabel nor the Peth-ick-Lawrences would keep a truce which meant no activity at all on their part. In April, when the Government launched a nationwide census, they advised their membership to resist it.

Why should they allow the Government to number them when they were not treated as citizens? Why should they submit financial and other information about themselves when they had no financial, professional or legal standing in the country?

"The census," Emmeline's published statement read, "is a numbering of people. Until women count as people for the purpose of representation in the councils of the nation as well as for purposes of taxation, we shall refuse to be numbered." She returned her own census form with the words boldly scrawled across it: *No vote, no census.*

This resistance programme caught on like wildfire. The most courageous women did the same as Emmeline,

though it invited fines or arrest. Others simply hid out
on the census day and avoided the census takers.

In Birmingham sixteen wealthy women with large
houses packed them from roofs to cellars with women
evading census day. The head of a women's school sheltered three hundred other defiant evaders. Others fled to
hotels or inns, or hired gypsy horse vans to escape out
into the country. And on the night when the census was
closed, the women returned and held parties and meetings and musicales to celebrate their passive-resistance
victory.

Significantly, not one woman was fined or arrested,
though such had been threatened. The Government
must have felt a trial would bring out political questions
too hot to handle.

✌ Chapter eight

The Conciliation Bill was debated on May 5, and this first reading passed the House, again by a large majority. It would have to go through a final reading. The Government stalled, saying it could not be brought up again until the autumn, after the summer recess.

No matter how many times Emmeline's hopes had been dashed, they rose again. *This time,* she thought. *Perhaps this time!*

She was fifty-three years old. She yearned for victory. She longed for that day when she would sit in the gallery of the House of Commons and see her daughter, the **Honourable** Christabel Harriette Pankhurst, take her seat as the first woman member.

It did not seem an unrealistic hope. What other woman was as trained and experienced in politics as Christabel? She had her degree in law. She had proved herself an able organizer, an adroit campaigner, a fearless speaker. Who else could claim so much?

Only to Christabel herself did her mother ever speak of this, and Christabel's answer was typical of her shrewd knowledge of people. If she ever did become a candidate, she said, there would certainly be two votes cast against her: Adela's and Sylvia's.

The dissension among the sisters simmered just below the surface. To the public they were a united family. They were all ardent suffragettes, and one was as often in the newspaper headlines as the others. If Adela was just coming out of gaol, Sylvia was just going in and Christabel in danger of it. Christabel was famous for her editorials in *Votes for Women,* but Sylvia had a flair for writing too, and had been commissioned by a publisher to write a suffragette history.

It was only in the rare times when the family was all in one place that the differences came out in family councils. Emmeline tried to be peacemaker, but to little avail.

Christabel had one goal, one purpose: votes for women. She was engaged in one battle—for women—and she recognized only one army, of women. Adela and Sylvia, on the other hand, worked more closely with working women than any others, and they thought that an eight-hour day and higher wages for women just as important as the vote —and that men and women should help each other.

Christabel was a feminist. She believed women were naturally finer, better, purer and more spiritual than men. When women came to power they would make the world a better place, and they didn't need men's help to do it. Though she was the prettiest of the sisters, she had never had a romance and didn't want one.

Adela and Sylvia were comfortable working with men, as well as with women. If they had no romances, it was only because they weren't out of gaol long enough to have time for them. Sylvia was so popular with the poor of the

East End that one big fellow had even appointed himself
her bodyguard and went with her to all public meetings.

Emmeline was pleased to see Sylvia change from a shy
and shrinking girl to a self-possessed young woman, but
the mother was not fully aware of the widening view-
points among her daughters. She was away too much. In
October of that year she again sailed for America, for
another triumphant speaking tour.

She was in Minneapolis in November, and it was there
that she picked up a newspaper and read that the Prime
Minister had killed the Conciliation Bill. He said there
was no time for it to be heard that session. It could not
be carried over into the spring session; a new bill would
have to be introduced and go through the same readings.

By now Emmeline should have been used to shattered
hopes, but it wasn't so. Each disappointment hit her
harder than the one before. She was stunned.

Her American friends asked why the Prime Minister
had done this, when the majority of the House seemed in
favour of woman suffrage. Was it just spite?

But Emmeline Pankhurst was no fool, and she understood politics. She could understand Mr. Asquith, though
she despised him all the more for it. He and the Cabinet
were afraid of such a radical change, afraid that their
Party might lose the next election over this issue. Mr.
Asquith's ear was hearing other voices than the suffragettes', or even those of the House of Commons. There
were factory owners, representing power and wealth, who
wanted no change in the status of women workers who
were now at their mercy. Some trade unions were reluc-
tant, fearing the "new woman" might compete with men

for jobs. Nor was Mr. Asquith sure that the majority of husbands and fathers wanted to give up the control they now had over their womenfolk.

None of this justified Asquith, in Emmeline's eyes. He had moral obligations as well as political ones.

When her ship reached England, she found that the truce was over. Suffragettes had reacted, spontaneously, in a mood of vengeful protest. Asquith's residence was besieged by women calling out: "Traitor!"

The W.S.P.U. had joined with the heads of other suffragette organizations in a delegation to the Prime Minister. This one he did not refuse to see, but he simply made excuses which satisfied no one.

Mrs. Pethick-Lawrence had been so outraged at his feeble excuses that she had led her own W.S.P.U. group out of the meeting and into a raid. With stones and hammers the W.S.P.U. women broke hundreds of windows in the Home Office, the War and Foreign Offices, the Board of Education, the Privy Council and other buildings.

The word had spread like magic that day. Hundreds of women, many having no affiliation with the W.S.P.U., joined Mrs. Pethick-Lawrence to wreak havoc all over London, especially up and down Whitehall and around government buildings. Two hundred and twenty were arrested, including Mrs. Lawrence, and one hundred and fifty were sentenced to prison for a week to two months.

Emmeline arrived shortly afterwards and added her approval to Christabel's editorials calling for force. The breaking of windows and destruction of property, she said, were time-honoured traditions in the history of English revolts Men had gathered together and smashed things, and even set fire to buildings, to get what they wanted when the Government denied them.

Well, women would do the same.

On February 16, 1912, at a huge meeting called to welcome home some of the released gaol prisoners, Emmeline stated her policy:

"If the argument of the stone, that time-honoured political weapon, is sufficient, then we will never use any stronger argument." Her audience caught its breath. By stronger argument did she mean the gun or the torch? But she only went on to speak of the stone. "That is the weapon and the argument we are going to use . . . because it is the easiest and the most readily understood. Why should women go to Parliament Square and be battered about and insulted and, most important, produce less effect than when they threw stones? We have tried this long enough. We submitted for years patiently to insult and assault. . . . Is not a woman's life, is not her health . . more valuable than panes of glass? Does not the breaking of glass produce more effect upon the Government? If you are fighting a battle, that should decide your choice of weapons."

She was cheered until throats were hoarse. Her troops were with her. The battle was joined; the firing line had been reached.

She was right in saying that the Government was alarmed. When she announced a demonstration for March 4, Sir William Boyles got up in Parliament to ask the Home Secretary whether his attention had been drawn to 'a speech by Mrs. Pankhurst last Friday night, openly inciting her hearers to violent outrage and destruction of property"—and what steps he proposed to take "to protect society from this outbreak of lawlessness?"

Plans were made for extra policemen to protect the homes and offices of Cabinet members on March 4. Shopkeepers near Parliament Square boarded up their glass windows and hired special patrol guards.

The planners at Clement's Inn outwitted them. The public announcement for the demonstration was for the 4th; but a private one to trusted W.S.P.U. members was for March 1. At exactly half-past five on the 1st Emmeline Pankhurst, Mrs. Tuke and another woman hurled stones at the windows of No. 10 Downing Street, the Prime Minister's residence. They were arrested, but not before the damage was done, and even as they were being escorted to the nearest police station another relay of women was hurling stones in another part of London.

No sooner were the police alerted to one section of London than the trouble broke out in an entirely different part. The suffragettes were no longer limiting themselves to government buildings but were also attacking shops and banks and post offices. If the Government wouldn't listen to them perhaps the Government would listen to an alarmed public.

The *Daily Mail* wrote the story of that March 1, and Emmeline read it the next morning. "From every part of the crowded and brilliantly lit streets came the crash of splintered glass. People started as a window shattered at their side; suddenly there was another crash in front of them; on the other side of the street—behind—everywhere. Scared shop assistants came running this way and that; five minutes later the streets were a procession of excited groups, each surrounding a woman wrecker being led in custody to the nearest police station. Shop windows rattled down. Lights in shop windows were suddenly extinguished."

The day, Emmeline thought with satisfaction, had been a brilliant success. It was a pity that the destruction hit the innocent as well as the guilty, but those shops and banks were owned and operated by male voters. If they wanted to keep their windows safe they could start exerting pressure on the Government to give the women what they wanted.

On March 4, unheard-of preparations were made around Parliament Square. Thousands of police were there, as if they expected a hostile, armed force to arrive. Shopkeepers barricaded their premises and removed goods out of shop windows. Offices hired special guards. Londoners jammed the streets all around the square area to see the advertised show. Mounted police rode up and down to control the crowd and intimidate the women when they showed up.

But they didn't show. Not one suffragette marched to the square. Not one stone was thrown.

The W.S.P.U. had made a clever feint. While the police were concentrated around Parliament Square, one hundred women gathered in Knightsbridge, another section of London, and were methodically going up and down streets there and smashing windows. Some were arrested, but most got safely away.

When the arrested women were brought into police

courts and lectured by outraged magistrates on the sacred-
ness of private property, the suffragettes' answers were reported in the newspapers:

"If the Government is deaf to our petitions, perhaps
they can hear the smashing of glass."

Emmeline Pankhurst was sentenced to two months'
imprisonment, as were most of the other two hundred
arrested women. Holloway Gaol was strained to the bursting point with the arrival of so many, and Emmeline led
the suffragettes inside gaol as ably as she led them when
free.

She and the others refused to obey prison rules. When
the wardresses tried to force them to wear the uniforms
and keep silent, the suffragettes went on a hunger strike.
Before Emmeline had begun to suffer any pangs of real
starvation, the Governor approached her and begged her
to call off the strike. She did so after he had promised
concessions.

As a result, the suffragettes were no longer coerced;
they could converse with each other on the exercise
ground, and their sentences were all shortened by many
days.

All except Emmeline's. While she was in gaol on this
charge, she was served with a warrant for another. She
and Mr. and Mrs. Pethick-Lawrence would have to stand
trial on the very serious charges of conspiring to commit
damage and injury to property, and aiding, abetting,
counselling and procuring the commission of offences
dealing with injuries to property.

The Pethick-Lawrences were held in prison without
bail while awaiting trial; like Emmeline, they had to pre-

pare for their defence from their cells, with only an occasional meeting with their lawyer. Mrs. Tuke had also been arrested, but she was shortly released when it was determined that her services at Clement's Inn had been mainly secretarial.

In the midst of this harried and anxious preparation for her trial, Emmeline learned from her lawyer of one brighter aspect. There had been a warrant out for Christabel's arrest too, but Christabel had escaped. She was in hiding, but she was still functioning. *Votes for Women* still carried her editorials.

The preliminary hearing began on March 14. Emmeline quickly realized that the prosecution was determined to avoid any political issues. The defendants were simply co-conspirators who had enticed other women to go out and do wilful damage to property for some sinister reason of their own.

The Pethick-Lawrences and Emmeline were finally released on bail, and the trial was to take place on May 15.

Just as soon as she was free, Emmeline sought out Annie Kenney. "Where is Christabel?" she asked. Annie, who delighted in intrigues, told her the story. Christabel had been warned that an arrest was due, and she had at first hidden out in the Pine-Townsend Nursing Home. It was not a safe place. She stayed there one night, then disguised herself and got out of London and over the Channel to Paris.

She and Annie were in constant correspondence. From Paris came a stream of directions for the work of the W.S.P.U.—material for leaflets and the editorials for the newspaper *Votes for Women.*

Emmeline was proud of her daughter. No matter what moves the police made to harass or silence the top leadership of the W.S.P.U., the work would go on. Even though the warrant was still out for Christabel's arrest, it was not likely that France would hand her over to the British Government—not if she restricted her activities to Britain and did not agitate in France. With able lieutenants like Annie Kenney, Christabel could carry on.

The Pethick-Lawrences were just as pleased. If they were found guilty in the coming trial, their sentences might be long ones. There was comfort in the thought that Christabel was free.

The trial by jury opened on May 15, as scheduled. The judge was Lord Coleridge. This was ironic, because his father, Sir Charles Coleridge, had appeared with Dr. Pankhurst in 1867 in a famous law case, where they had tried to prove that women were entitled to the vote! Now the son sat in judgment over two women deprived of that right.

Sir Rufus Isaacs tried hard to keep woman suffrage out of the trial. In his opening address to the jury he said: "I am very anxious to impress upon you from the moment we begin . . . that all questions of whether a woman is entitled to the Parliamentary franchise . . . are questions which are in no sense involved in the trial of this issue. . . ."

Emmeline looked around the room at the robed judge on the bench, at the all-male jury, at the lawyers in their black silk robes, at the spectators. Did any one of them really believe Sir Rufus?

But the judge upheld the prosecution, and so Mr.

Healey, the defence lawyer, was hampered during examination and cross-examination. He could not bring out
anything about *why* the windows were smashed, nor could
he deny that the defendants had organized and planned
the demonstration. It was understood between lawyer
and defendants that everything would depend upon the
speeches each of the three would make from the dock.
Traditionally, a defendant pleading for himself was
granted a lot more freedom in what he said than in what
his lawyer could say for him.

On May 20 the examinations were over and Mr. Pethick-Lawrence rose to speak. He was impressive. He said:

". . . The case that I have to put before you is that
neither the conspiracy nor the incitement to it is ours;
but that the conspiracy is a conspiracy of the Cabinet
which is responsible for the government of this country;
and that the incitement is the incitement of the Ministers
of the Crown. . . . If these **honourable** gentlemen had
shown that they were prepared to listen to reason and to
argument . . . these events which you have so patiently
listened to during these days would never have taken
place."

This was the heart of the defence. The Government
should be on trial, not they. Pethick-Lawrence went on
to expose the "humbug," as he called it, of the Government's promises, its pretence to agree with the suffragettes
and its conspiracy to kill any bill on woman suffrage.

Should the women be blamed if they were no
longer patient when the Government could no longer
be trusted? Pethick-Lawrence hammered home this point.

He and the two women sitting behind him were

strange "criminals" to be found in the raised prisoners'
dock of a police court. Mr. Pethick-Lawrence (he was one
day to be raised to the peerage and become Lord Pethick-
Lawrence) was not only a handsome man, but one whose
legal reputation outshone both judge and prosecutor.
His wife's good breeding was obvious, and her charm
abundant.

Of the three of them, only Emmeline looked capable
of hurling stones. In spite of her greying hair, there was
no softening of age in her face. She was thin, and her
great, greenish eyes were like those of a hawk, shadowed
dark below them. The beautiful bones of her chin and
temples and cheekbones were sharply visible, no longer
sweet in their curves, but carrying the very stamp of
haughty courage and strength.

In her own defence speech she quoted an old statement
of Lloyd George's. "There comes a time in the life of
a people suffering from an intolerable injustice when the
only way to maintain one's self-respect is to revolt against
that injustice." She paused. Silence grew in the courtroom until at last she added: "That time came for us."

"Year after year"—she had the trick of keeping her
voice low, so that there was not the slightest noise in the
courtroom as everyone strained to hear—"month after
month, the fate of women is decided. How they are to
live, their relationship with their children, the marriage
laws under which they are joined in union and pledge
their affections . . . and women have no voice." Again
she paused and looked straight and unafraid at the jury.
"We will fight until we are given that voice."

Since the defendants admitted organizing the demonstrations of March 1 and 4, the jury had to call them guilty. But the defence speeches had had their effect. The jury added this recommendation to their verdict:

"The jurymen unanimously desire to express the hope that, taking into consideration the undoubtedly pure motives which underlie the agitation that has led to this trouble, you will be pleased to exercise the utmost clemency and leniency."

It was a direct request to the judge to suspend sentences, but the judge was not so inclined. He would not be lenient. He sentenced all three, as common criminals, to nine months in jail—an unwonted harshness.

Emmeline, as she stood to hear judgment pronounced upon her, was in no mood to accept that sentence. What she wanted to do was what her husband had asked her a long time ago, scratch their eyes out. She could not do that, but neither was she going to serve nine months in gaol.

Immediately, when they found themselves in adjoining cells in Holloway, she and Mrs. Pethick-Lawrence went on a hunger strike. So did Mr. Pethick-Lawrence in the men's prison.

This weapon, one that was virtually self-destruction, was one Emmeline would have preferred that only mature women use. She had a horror of this agony for young girls—but she could not prevent their following her lead. As soon as it was known that Mrs. Pankhurst was refusing food, other suffragette prisoners in Holloway and other prisons did the same.

The first days were not too terrible. Emmeline lay on her bed and gritted her teeth to suffer through the pangs in her stomach and the torture to her nerves. Then came the days of drifting into a state of half-dreams and near-hallucinations, terrible weakness and burning fever. Food —hot and spicy and sweet—was brought into her cell and placed close to her bed.

Sometimes she forgot why she was depriving herself of food. Sometimes she was just annoyed at herself for being so weak that she could not stretch out her hand for the food, and she would do so, feebly touching the dish before she remembered and fell back on her bed and turned her face to the wall.

This was the longest she had ever gone without food. Was it to end in death? Would the authorities really let her die rather than give in? She faced this possibility too. She would die then. She would not be the first martyr to the cause.

At times, in her fever and her state of semiconscious stupor, she could not be sure of what was real and what was not—whether she was hearing real voices or just ones in her head. One night she heard screaming from many parts of the jail. The dreadful sounds seemed to be coming from her floor and from below it.

She dragged herself off the bed and crawled to the door and crouched there, listening. Yes, the sounds were real ones. There was the thud of many boots, which had to be the wardresses'; there was the screech of keys opening doors, then voices and protests. Emmeline heard a man shout: "We'll *make* you eat!" and then, again, that terrible, awful screaming of a woman prisoner.

The suffragettes were being force-fed. Shuddering, Emmeline suffered along with the sufferers.

Then, from Mrs. Pethick-Lawrence's cell came her thin, weak voice, and she was *singing!* She was singing the words of the suffragette song:

"Shout, shout—up with your song,

"Cry with the wind, for the dawn is breaking. . . ."

Tears flowed down Emmeline's wasted cheeks as from all over the gaol came other feeble voices joining in, and she whispered the words along with them:

"March, march, swing you along,

"Wide blows our banner and hope is waking . . ."

"Silence!" cried out the wardresses, but the women would not be silent. They sang on and on, throughout the night, to cheer and encourage each other and to give what little comfort they could to those who were being visited by the doctor and his instruments of torture.

It was the next afternoon, following that sleepless night and a morning of acute pain in her muscles and nerves, that Emmeline heard a commotion next door and then a cry of horror and protest. Instantly she knew what was happening. There were thumps, as if a stool had been knocked over, and screams from Mrs. Pethick-Lawrence. The force-feeding was going on there, and it would be Emmeline's turn next.

From somewhere she found the strength to stand up. She braced her back against the wall and put her hand on the only weapon in the cell, a heavy earthenware jug for water. Then she waited. Soon she heard the cell door next to hers open and slam shut, and then footsteps coming to her. The key was turned and the door flung wide.

There stood two heavy-set wardresses, a doctor and a

big male assistant. The doctor was carrying the coiled rubber tube with its sharp, steel-pointed opening, used to pry clenched teeth apart. He took a step forward.

Emmeline raised the jug. "If any of you dares so much as to take one step into this cell, I shall defend myself," she declared.

It should have been laughable. She was one person against four. She was a pitiful skeleton defying four strong and healthy trained people. She could barely lift the jug in her shaking hands. Yet they did not laugh and they did not move. There was such a moral force about her that they were cowed. They were daunted. They could not look at those burning eyes.

The doctor turned away first, muttering. His assistant hung his head and followed. The wardresses were about to trail after them when Emmeline stopped them.

"Take me to Mrs. Pethick-Lawrence. I want to see for myself what you have done to her."

Why did they agree? Even they did not know. They only knew that Emmeline Pankhurst would not, could not, be refused, and they found themselves obeying her. One took her key from her pocket and went to the next cell and unlocked the door; the other offered Emmeline an arm to help her walk, and then stood aside to let her enter.

When Emmeline saw the figure on the bed, moaning and bleeding, she angrily shook off the wardress' hand. She made her own way to Mrs. Pethick-Lawrence's side and sank down on the bed and took that lovely head on her lap. It was not so lovely now. Blood was trickling

down from her nose and mouth. Her hair was wet and
matted. The liquid soup had spilled over her chin and
neck, adding its mess to the blood and vomit.

Her lips were cut and swollen, but she managed to
whisper what had happened. She had not expected them
today, and they had rushed on her before she could prepare herself. Yet she had struggled and had clenched her
teeth and lips tight. The wardress had tried to pry them
open; when that failed, the doctor had brutally, ruthlessly
forced the steel point of the tube between her teeth and
the tube down her throat.

The liquid food had flooded the passages of her nose
and throat, suffocating and gagging her. The doctor
did not care, just so long as a little of it went into her
stomach.

Emmeline held the basin for her while she retched,
and wiped the blood off her face. Then Mrs. Pethick-
Lawrence fainted. Emmeline turned to the wardresses,
who were still standing in the doorway. "You will never
touch her again," she commanded them.

And they never did. Neither Emmeline nor Mrs.
Pethick-Lawrence were ever visited again by the doctor
and his feeding apparatus. And both women were so
near starvation that they were released within a couple
of days. At a terrible cost to themselves, they had succeeded in doing what they had said they would—flouting
the court and its verdict and sentence.

So were all the other suffragette prisoners released,
one after another. The Governor of Holloway was afraid
of a death on his hands.

When Emmeline was freed, she found there had been

a storm of world-wide publicity about her trial, the hunger strikes and the forced feeding. International societies of all kinds, prominent individuals of many nations and even government bodies sent protests to the British Government. One such request to free Mrs. Pankhurst and the other suffragettes was signed by Professor Paul Milyoukoff, President of the Russian Duma; Enrico Ferri, of the Italian Chamber of Deputies; Madame Curie, the discoverer of radium; Maurice Maeterlinck, the famous writer; and many other eminent persons.

The greatest uproar was in the House of Commons. Descriptions of the brutality of forced feeding had shocked parliamentarians. On the floor of the House there was a stormy questioning of the Prime Minister and the Home Secretary. Mr. Asquith was made to answer, and he said: "I must point out this, that there is not one single prisoner who cannot go out of prison this afternoon on giving the undertaking asked for by the Home Secretary." The "undertaking" meant a signed pledge not to engage in militant suffrage work.

George Lansbury, a member of the House, jumped to his feet and shouted: "You know they cannot! It is perfectly disgraceful that the Prime Minister of England should make such a statement!"

Mr. Asquith sat down, silent, but George Lansbury was not finished with him. Lansbury strode down the aisle to confront the Prime Minister and say, "That was a disgraceful thing for you to say, Sir. You are beneath contempt, you and your colleagues. . . . You will go down in history as the men who tortured innocent women!"

The entire House seethed with cries of "Shame!"—
some directed against the Prime Minister, some against
Lansbury for what they considered his most ungentle-
manly behaviour Mr. Asquith sharply ordered Lansbury
to leave the House for the day, and Lansbury shouted
back at him:

"You murder, torture and drive women mad, and then
you tell them they can walk out. You ought to be driven
out of public life! These women are showing you what
principle is. You ought to honour them for standing up
for their principles." He stepped back, turned and addressed the whole House. "I tell you, Commons of England, you ought to be ashamed of yourselves!"

Emmeline Pankhurst found she was a heroine.

⌁ Chapter nine

Emmeline and Mrs. Pethick-Lawrence had to be carried out of gaol, but a few days in the Nursing Home brought back enough health and strength so that Mrs. Pethick-Lawrence could go to her country home to recuperate and Emmeline could go to Paris.

The sudden change from the horrors she had so recently endured to the gaiety of the French capital city, from cell to hospital bed to Christabel's charming and feminine apartment and from no food to soups and gruels and then to her favourite French cooking left Emmeline in a daze at first. But it was just the change she needed, and she quickly blossomed in it.

From the days of her French finishing school when she had been a young girl, Emmeline had loved Paris and all its frivolous, elegant ways. This was the other side of her nature, which only Christabel, of all her daughters, shared with her. Now, with gratitude, Emmeline put Holloway out of her mind and let herself be pampered and spoon-fed by Christabel's maid, Berthé, and slept late in the mornings between clean, silky sheets.

When she first arrived, her appearance had terrified

Berthé. Emmeline was emaciated; her skin was yellow, the flesh of her face and hands barely covering the sharp bones. But she quickly gained a few pounds, and her colouring improved, although the great, dark circles under her eyes remained, and her general health was never as good as before.

Christabel's apartment on the Avenue de la Grande Armée was a beehive of activity, a remote command post. Her letters to London and her editorials went out in every post; every week, at least, Annie Kenney or another lieutenant crossed the English Channel to report and receive orders. Yet Christabel had time to make important friends. As soon as Emmeline was better, she went with her daughter to the drawing room of the Princess de Polignac, and was proud to see Christabel the centre of attention among titled Parisian intellectuals.

Emmeline's days in Paris were a glorious holiday from the embattled work in London. She strolled in the park, rode in a hansom cab down the Champs Elysées, sat with Christabel in fashionable cafés or walked slowly past the famous dressmakers of the Rue de la Paix, indulging her weakness of window shopping

It was not all play. She and Christabel had long talks about the future of the suffrage movement in Britain. Christabel was elated at the world-wide publicity which the stone-throwing demonstrations and the subsequent arrests had received. Peaceful protests and the marches to Parliament had become routine, she felt; they were no longer news.

Therefore the programme for the future would be to

step up the actual, physical warfare. The Government must be publicly brought to its knees. Christabel was scornful of the efforts of even such men as Keir Hardie and George Lansbury inside the House. She envisioned an army of women, aroused and militant, taking matters into their own hands and wreaking such destruction of property on such an increased scale that the Government would have to capitulate. Christabel thought in terms of actual warfare—though she stopped short of gunfire.

Emmeline was easily persuaded. It had been Christabel's single-minded drive and logic that had taken them this far, that had shaken the suffrage movement out of its passive doldrums, and the mother thought there had never been such a brilliant leader as her oldest daughter.

There were other problems to discuss, which concerned the younger daughters. Christabel was sharply critical of Adela and almost as much so of Sylvia.

Adela had become a full-time worker for the W.S.P.U., travelling all over the country to speak and agitate, but her activities did not contain themselves in the narrow limits which Christabel demanded for W.S.P.U. members. She spoke at Liberal Party, Labour Party and Socialist meetings, and supported their candidates on all sorts of issues besides that of woman suffrage.

"But the worst," said Christabel wrathfully, "is the report I have just heard. Yorkshire textile workers are on strike. Adela is not only supporting them, but she has the whole local W.S.P.U. branch spending all its time helping the strikers instead of concentrating on our cause. She must be stopped."

"I'll speak to her," Emmeline promised.

However, she was not so willing to take action against Sylvia, though Christabel pressed for it.

"She won't work anywhere but the East End," said Christabel, "and she has even moved there, into the poorest slum rooms she could find. She claims that, by moving the suffrage cause out of drawing rooms and into the slums, she is building a truly mass base of active women. I wouldn't worry so much about her nonsense, but she's getting money from our wealthier W.S.P.U. branches to open headquarters in what she calls 'her' districts, and some of our best workers—such as Lady Sybil Smith and Evelina Haverfield, the daughter of Lord Abinger—are helping her."

Over the years, Emmeline had grown more and more conservative until, finally, her only radical activity was for votes for women. She distrusted Sylvia's desire to change the lot of poor working people as much as Christabel did, but she was cautious. "The Pethick-Lawrences highly approve of Sylvia's work. And you must admit that she is always able to lead a large group to every one of our demonstrations, where numbers count."

What she did not say to Christabel was that she was becoming aware the two daughters were rivals. The change in Sylvia was spectacular; she had become a fearless leader and speaker. It was Sylvia, *not* Christabel, who had just published a book on woman suffrage, and who had just returned from a most successful speaking tour in America.

Sylvia's rise to popularity and prominence was a challenge to Christabel's top place in the W.S.P.U., and the mother could only hope to keep peace between the two of them.

When Emmeline returned to London, family matters had to wait on a more important matter. This was the declaration of war which she and Christabel had drawn up. It was published in their newspaper, sent to the large daily commercial newspapers and issued in thousands of leaflets.

It read: "The leaders of the Women's Social and Political Union have so often warned the Government that unless the vote were granted to women in response to the mild militancy of the past, a fiercer spirit of revolt would be awakened which it would be impossible to control. The Government have blindly disregarded the warning, and now they are reaping the harvest of their unstatesmanlike folly."

The "spirit of revolt" needed only that declaration to burst into flame. Women all over Britain did not need to be told what to do; they invented their own plots and their own weapons. A hatchet was thrown into Mr. Asquith's car when it was empty. Two women set the Theatre Royal in Dublin on fire; windows were smashed in the country homes of members of Parliament.

One woman visited a golf course where it was known that wealthy politicians played. She burned into the green turf with acid the words *Votes for Women*. This began a whole series of raids on golf courses; even the royal golf links at Balmoral Castle in Scotland were not spared. In the dead of night, women replaced all the usual flags on the marking sticks with W.S.P.U. flags or with signs that read: "Forcible feedings must stop."

Historic buildings and post offices were disfigured with tar and acid. Travellers found barricades set up on roads and bridges, hung with W.S.P.U. signs and slogans. But gradually, it was the torch that became the most popular and frightening weapon. Women learned when the families and servants of House of Commons members would be away from home, then tried to burn down their houses. Guards at picture galleries and historical monuments were alerted, but women set fire to them anyway. None were burned to the ground, but damage was done.

The declaration issued, Emmeline had time to see Adela. She found her youngest daughter so ill from overwork that Adela had no strength to resist her. Emmeline offered her a bargain: she would pay for a course for Adela at the Studley Horticultural College if the girl would promise to refrain from politics of any kind. In a state of physical collapse, Adela yearned for the peace of handling only plants and flowers and she rashly gave her promise.

But Emmeline was faced with a revolt far worse than Adela's.

Mr. and Mrs. Pethick-Lawrence were horrified at the results of the declaration of war. They were militants; they wanted action in the struggle for woman suffrage; they had proved they were not cowards. They were, however, opposed to what they called "senseless destruction" of property, which they felt served no purpose but to drive public sympathy away from the W.S.P.U. And Sylvia agreed with them.

The conflict in the leadership came to a head. The Pethick-Lawrences and Emmeline crossed over to France and met Christabel at Boulogne. For days they argued, walking up and down the windy headlands that over-looked the sea. It was a time of deepest distress for them all, for the Pethick-Lawrences had loved Christabel as their own daughter.

Yet they thought her policy was wrong. The W.S.P.U., when the Pethick-Lawrences and Emmeline had last emerged from gaol, held the pulse of public sympathy—and now they were rapidly losing it. Their own willing-ness to sacrifice themselves brought support for suffrage; vengeful acts of destruction hardened hostility to them.

"We must look for new and imaginative actions which will draw people to co-operate with us," they said. "Per-haps the time has come to make alliances, especially with the men's organizations which are trying to extend male suffrage to all men. Sylvia thinks so, too."

Christabel only grew more and more adamant as the arguments went on. She would not yield. What were these new methods, these new alliances? They were only a rejection of everything the W.S.P.U. stood for. Hadn't she always said they were committed to warfare? They could not retreat, now that the battle was truly joined.

Emmeline saw, sadly, that there could be no compro-mise. She was, of course, heart and soul behind whatever Christabel proposed. It would be unthinkable for her to side with anyone against her daughter. Emmeline Pankhurst firmly believed that it was Christabel's genius which would surely lead them to victory.

The disagreement at Boulogne widened until it be-came a split. There was no other way. In the autumn of 1912 there appeared a new newspaper called *The*

Suffragette, since *Votes for Women* was owned by Mr.
Pethick-Lawrence. And in both papers there was an
identical announcement headed "Grave Statement by
the Leaders." It read:

"At the first reunion of the leaders after the enforced
holiday, Mrs. Pankhurst and Miss Christabel Pankhurst
outlined a new militant policy which Mr. and Mrs.
Pethick-Lawrence found themselves altogether unable to
support.

"Mrs. Pankhurst and Miss Christabel Pankhurst indi-
cated that they were not prepared to modify their inten-
tions, and recommended that Mr. and Mrs. Pethick-
Lawrence should resume control of the paper, *Votes for
Women,* and should leave the Women's Social and Political Union.

"Rather than make schism in the ranks of the Union
Mr. and Mrs. Pethick-Lawrence consented to take this
course."

It was signed by all four leaders.

The Pethick-Lawrences joined Mrs. Despard's Wom-
en's Freedom League, and some former W.S.P.U. members followed them. In private, Sylvia argued with her
mother that the Pethick-Lawrences were right and Christabel too inflexible, although in public she said no word
of criticism. Annie Kenney, on the other hand, staunchly
declared that "if all the world were on one side, and
Christabel Pankhurst on the other, I would walk straight
over to Christabel Pankhurst!"

There were so many murmurings and questionings in
the ranks that Emmeline called a large meeting of all
the W.S.P.U. London branches, to give them a fuller

explanation. As she sat in the chairman's seat and waited
for the moment to begin the meeting, she saw that, for
the first time in many years, there were empty seats here
and there.

The sight of them angered her. Emmeline was growing more and more imperious as she grew older and less
and less inclined to accept the implied criticism of those
empty seats.

The applause that greeted her as she stood up reas-
sured her. If the numbers were smaller, those who remained were the valiant, the strong and the faithful.
Emmeline began her speech by praising the Pethick-
Lawrences for their "incalculable services" but declaring
that "we of the W.S.P.U. shall continue the militant
agitation."

"There is a great deal of criticism of this movement,"
she said, acknowledging the adverse publicity they were
getting, "criticism from gentlemen who do not hesitate
to order out armies to kill . . . who do not hesitate to
encourage mobs to attack defenceless women. There is
something that governments care far more for than human life, and that is the security of property, and so it is
through property that we shall strike the enemy. . . ."

"Be militant," she advised the women, "each in your
own way. And my last word is to the Government: I
INCITE THIS MEETING TO REBELLION!"

Although a few women sat and would not respond,
the rest were on their feet and cheering lustily. And in
the weeks following that speech of Emmeline's, violence
erupted all over the country, in renewed and fiercer
forms. *Each in your own way*—Emmeline had removed

all controls and discipline and encouraged the suffragettes to rise to more and more daring exploits.

As government buildings, the post offices became favourite targets all over Britain. Acids were poured into the letter slots; chemicals were slipped inside the letter boxes, bursting into flame and consuming the contents; black fluids were poured in to ruin letters and packages. The Government, appalled, reckoned that over 5,000 letters were destroyed and many others delayed in transit.

Though retaliations were swift and many women were arrested, it did seem at that time that the Pankhurst policy was to succeed. Late in 1912 a vague promise was made that the Male Franchise Bill (to extend the vote to more men) would be heard in the new session, and that an amendment could be made to it to include women. Sir Edward Grey moved the amendment, and it was accepted.

Immediately Emmeline called a truce to violence. The suffragettes would suspend the war until the hearing of the bill in January, 1913.

Emmeline was glad of the respite. She needed this time to handle a most serious problem. It was no longer possible for her to ignore Christabel's warnings about Sylvia; in just a few months it had become plain that Sylvia was leading "her" women along a different path— one which Emmeline could not approve.

The East End Federation, as Sylvia called her W.S.P.U. branch, was not only draining money and workers from the W.S.P.U. headquarters, but concerning itself with such things as child nurseries, higher wages, equal pay for women and improvement of slum housing.

The straw that broke Christabel's patience was Sylvia's publication of her own newspaper: *Women's Dreadnought*. Very well written, it was a challenge to the official W.S.P.U. paper. Christabel and Emmeline conferred in Paris, and then sent for Sylvia to come and explain herself.

From the moment Sylvia walked into Christabel's luxurious apartment there was tension. The younger sister was thin and wasted from her last prison ordeal; she was shabbily dressed; her manner was belligerent, showing her scorn for her sister's comfortable life and her servant and her rich friends.

Christabel's plump cheeks reddened with anger. She was not used to such contempt, and she immediately laid down the law. Sylvia's East End organization was being supported by funds from other W.S.P.U. branches, and that would be stopped immediately and finally unless Sylvia stopped publishing socialist nonsense in her newspaper. She was to concentrate on woman suffrage and nothing else.

"Your work in the East End is along the wrong lines. We cannot have it," Christabel said with arrogance.

Sylvia protested hotly, and the two sisters went at it, hammer and tongs, while their mother watched them both with the most anxious feelings. Adela had capitulated to her authority, but she had a foreboding that this new Sylvia would not tamely submit.

"My work in the East End," Sylvia was insisting, "is proving itself to be right. The women want the vote, and they'll make sacrifices for it, far more than wealthy women who have servants to care for their homes and children while they campaign, and who go back from prison to luxury. But poor women also want to know that I'll fight for higher wages for them and their husbands, and for good housing instead of the slums they live in. And—yes—I'll work with men's organizations, and when they find we care about their problems then they are willing to help us."

Christabel was scornful. "Working women are of no value to us," she declared. "They are the weakest of their sex. How can it be otherwise, when their lives are so hard, their education so meagre? We want picked women, the very strongest and most intelligent."

Angry tears came into Sylvia's eyes. "You don't know those women and the strength in them! Why are we struggling for the vote if it is not to improve conditions for working women? That is what Father wanted, and Keir Hardie, and it is what I want."

"There will be no socialism in the W.S.P.U." Christabel stood up. Her mouth had hardened. She looked to her mother for support, and so did Sylvia. It was a moment of decision.

Emmeline knew it. She did not like to be reminded of her late husband's views, since her own had changed. At heart she was a middle-class, conservative woman. Like Christabel, she had come to believe that wealthy and educated women would do best with the vote, when they could then institute some benevolent reforms for the poor.

Yet she feared the determination in Sylvia. This daughter was no longer a timid girl. She was thirty-one years old. Emmeline temporized, saying, "Suppose I were to

say we would allow you something for your federation—
a little financial support."

Instantly Christabel became ruthless. "Oh, no! We
can't have that! It must be a clean cut."

By her silence Emmeline agreed, and now they both
looked at Sylvia. It was up to her. She could drop her
revolt and give up her federation and her newspaper and
stay in the W.S.P.U. under their domination—or refuse
and be on her own.

Slowly Sylvia got to her feet, looked at her mother in
one last, wordless appeal and then walked out of the
room. The Pankhurst family unity was broken.

The news created a minor sensation in London, and
Christabel silenced the gossip with a sharp editorial in
The Suffragette:

". . . Since the W.S.P.U. . . . is a fighting organization, it must have only one policy, one programme and
one command. The W.S.P.U. policy and the programme
are framed, and the word of command is given by Mrs.
Pankhurst and myself. Those who wish to give an independent lead . . . must necessarily have an independent
organization of their own."

In other words: *do as we tell you or get out.* Some
members did leave, but those who remained became
more intensely loyal to the Pankhurst mother and daughter than before. They spoke of Emmeline as their Queen.
They vaunted her courage above their own, although all
had suffered arrests and hunger strikes and forced feedings in prison. It was a time of great emotion, and some
of their meetings were held in a hysterical fervour.

When the new session of Parliament opened in Janu-

ary, the promise of votes for women was again defeated
in spite of all that Keir Hardie and George Lansbury
could do.

Emmeline declared the truce at an end, and the
W.S.P.U. went on a second and worse rampage of burning and wrecking all over the country. They cut tele-
graph and telephone wires and, at one time, all communication between London and Glasgow, Scotland, was
severed for hours. The greenhouse that sheltered the
rare orchids at Kew Gardens was smashed. Windows of
men's private clubs were broken. The glass case which
held the Crown Jewels in the Tower of London was
cracked open.

In this guerrilla warfare, the main focus of attack was
against government buildings, but suffragettes were also
angry that the Church of England had not helped them
and frequently preached against them. They invaded
Lambeth Palace, the residence of the Archbishop of
Canterbury, and broke the palace windows.

Then a new, uncompleted and empty home which
was being built for David Lloyd George was bombed.
Four days later Emmeline Pankhurst was arrested on the
charge of having "counselled and procured" the unknown
persons who had done this damage. It was not claimed
that she had set the bomb off herself, but that she had
incited others to do so.

The trial was set for April in the awesome Old Bailey,
where major crimes were tried.

Knowing the ordeal that lay ahead of her, Emmeline
went to Paris for a brief holiday. The small comforts and
luxuries which Christabel could offer her were more

than welcome. Her spirit had not flagged, but her body shrank from the agony she knew lay ahead. She had come to Paris straight from Sylvia's bedside, and she knew.

Sylvia had just been released from Holloway after an East End demonstration and arrest, and Emmeline had never seen such a pitiable sight. Sylvia's mouth was torn from the instrument of forced feeding. She was little more than skin and bones after her fast without food or water. She had even denied herself sleep, and she had whispered to her mother that, at times in Holloway, she was sure she was going mad.

This same torment of the flesh lay ahead of Emmeline, for she was certain that the trial would end in prison for her. Yet neither she nor Christabel could see any other way to their goal than to increase the violence and suffer the consequences.

The suffragettes of that day, and historians of the future, would argue long over this time of extreme violence. Was it effective, or did it delay the victory? Certainly the violence kept the question of suffrage prominent in the newspapers and in the minds of people; it was a relentless pressure upon the Government. But could this also have been accomplished in other ways?

Neither Christabel nor Emmeline thought there were other ways. They were single-minded. They were inflexible. Christabel even refused to work with a group of men who had organized themselves for woman suffrage, because they counselled other tactics.

The trial at Old Bailey opened on Wednesday, April 2, 1913, and the outcome was never in doubt. The jury found Emmeline guilty under the Malicious Damages to Property Act. Even so, the sentence of three years' penal servitude was monstrously severe. The courtroom was in an uproar when Justice Lush handed down his verdict and sentence.

It triggered worse outbreaks of violence. From one end of the British Isles to the other, women wreaked vengeance. Country mansions were set on fire; the Ayr race course grandstand was burned to the ground. A bomb was set off in Oxted Station, blowing out walls and windows. Empty railway carriages were fired and destroyed.

The Government had to close the British Museum, the National Gallery, Windsor Castle and other places where there were priceless paintings or objects of historical interest to public viewing. The W.S.P.U. members and sympathizers were careful not to endanger human life, but they were a constant threat to rare works of art.

Meanwhile, Emmeline had gone on a hunger-and-thirst strike as soon as she was in Holloway. The prison Governor did not dare to have her force-fed; the Government was afraid that her devoted followers would think of new ways of vengeance. Since Mrs. Pankhurst would either have to be released or die in gaol, a new law was passed in Parliament aimed directly at her.

This became commonly known as the Cat-and-Mouse Act. The Government and police were the cats; the suffragettes were the mice, whom they played with, pretending to release them only to snatch them back again.

Under the act, Emmeline was released from Holloway, but only for fifteen days, just time enough for her to

regain her health. Then the police could take her back
to prison to serve out her sentence. The same in-and-out
persecution applied to the suffragettes gaoled for acts of
destruction.

From the summer of 1913 Emmeline's life followed
this pattern. Her days inside Holloway grew shorter; her
time allowed outside, before the police pounced, grew
longer and even allowed her to make another trip to
America. This was not done out of generosity to her,
but out of fear. The hunger strikes were dangerous to
health. Going without water for several days was close
to suicide.

Each time Emmeline came out of prison and was pho-
tographed for newspapers, she generated a feeling of
national shame that a woman must treat herself so for
a cause. The Government seemed unnaturally cruel.
Every cell in her body had dried out until her flesh was
mummified. Her yellow skin was stretched tight over
bones that had become sharp and thin and brittle. Her
tongue was so swollen that she could not speak; if she
could walk at all, she tottered along like an ancient
crone.

Only a woman of unusual physical and moral forti-
tude could have endured this and then gone back to
endure more. Only a woman who had been born with
great beauty could have kept the remnants of that beauty
in spite of her suffering. If at times she looked like a
death's head, the exquisite shape was still there, and if
her dress hung about her starving body when she was
released, still it was velvet and had style.

But in 1913 something happened which affected her

far more deeply than her own bodily pains. One of her "splendid ones," as she called her followers, was killed.

To dramatize and call attention to the suffrage cause, Emily Wilding-Davison had thrown herself in front of the leading horse at the Derby Day horse-race. The horse had stumbled and fallen upon her, injuring her so terribly that she never regained consciousness.

~//~ Chapter ten

It had always been a torture to Emmeline to know that young girl suffragettes were undergoing even worse sufferings in gaol than she had to endure. "It is all very well for me," she told friends, "but not for them." All the limelight of publicity was centered on her, while the others' sacrifices went unheralded and unsung.

Not even her pity for them, nor the death of Miss Emily Wilding-Davison, however, would have been enough to make her put a stop to the militancy. In a war, some must fall. In the summer of 1914, Emmeline's troops had never been stauncher; they were ready to hurl themselves into greater and greater efforts; their devotion to her was passionate. She had only to speak and they would obey.

In spite of the horror the newspapers expressed at the bombings and burnings, the smashings and acid throwing, there were signs that the suffrage cause was winning. The signs were curious ones. There was still strong opposition, but the tone of that opposition had changed greatly. No longer was woman suffrage dismissed as a "crank" notion, put forward by "crank" women. It

could no longer be laughed at. It was a major and serious
political issue.

Yet, in August of 1914, Emmeline and Christabel for-
mally declared an end to *their* war, because another war
had broken out which they felt was far more important.
Germany had invaded Belgium. Britain and France had
then allied themselves with Belgium against Germany.
It was the outbreak of World War I.

The Pankhurst announcement not only astonished people, it amazed them. How to explain such an about-face
from Emmeline and Christabel, who had declared that
their own war would never end until they had what they
wanted?

Undoubtedly the death of Emily Wilding-Davison had
something to do with it, but the Pankhursts had faced
the possibility of deaths. Emmeline, herself, had come
close to it in hunger strikes. Fear of consequences had
not changed the Pankhurst mother and daughter; their
patriotism had, and their marvellous sense of timing.

For someone who had so long fought the Government,
Emmeline was actually an intensely patriotic woman,
loving her country, her King, Church and State—even
the snobbery of the English class system. As an English-
woman she would quarrel with her Government, but no
German was to threaten it. Outraged, Emmeline grasped
the Union Jack, put away the W.S.P.U. flag, and marched
out into a different war, still leading women.

Her dramatic flair again pushed her into the limelight.
With a whole nation roused to war fervour, the cause of
woman suffrage was forgotten by public and newspapers
alike. Rather than sink with one cause, Emmeline rode

the crest of another. She was among the first to lead marches and demonstrations, but her banners and slogans and songs had changed. Down the streets she led women, and suddenly everyone was cheering her. Even the police smiled upon her. Emmeline Pankhurst became the gallant symbol of Britain's womanhood, prepared to sacrifice everything for her country, to work unselfishly for victory.

To the amazement and delight of the Government, she was now speaking to her huge audience of women on their patriotic duty to forget, temporarily, woman suffrage. They must do everything they could *for* the Government now, instead of against it. And her faithful followers obeyed. The stone, the bottle of acid and the torch were laid down, and the women picked up knitting needles instead, to make scarves for soldiers.

Her old enemy Lloyd George, who was now Minister of Munitions, invited Emmeline Pankhurst to a secret conference. He confided in her the great need for women workers. The difficulty was, he explained, that the prevailing idea in Parliament was that women would not want to work, and would not want to leave their sheltered homes for the rough life of a factory.

Could Mrs. Pankhurst organize a great demonstration and march of women, *demanding* of Mr. Lloyd George that they be allowed to work? He would pretend to know nothing about it until it happened; he would be astonished by it; he could then go before Parliament and say that it was not he but the women of Britain who insisted on their patriotic right to work in war factories.

With plenty of Government money behind her, it was

child's play for Emmeline to organize the mass demonstration. Flaunting banners reading *Women's Right to
Serve,* thousands and thousands of women marched behind Emmeline to Parliament Square. This time there
were no police. The leaders were warmly received by
Lloyd George and Winston Churchill, who promised to
do everything they could to help women get into factories.

It was cynical politicking, but it was to have an effect
neither of those two politicians foresaw. The rush of so
many women into war jobs was like the breaking of a
dam. The old notions that women were too fragile, too
stupid and too inefficient to compete with men in skills
or intelligence were swept away.

Women not only did magnificent work in factories,
but they also invaded offices and professions. Whenever
a man left for the war front, a woman stepped into his
place, and these women showed by their excellence that
the prejudice against them had no basis in fact.

While Emmeline was enlisting the W.S.P.U. and thousands of other women behind her programme of "industrial
peace," which meant that workers were to be content
with small wages to help the war effort, Christabel was
lecturing in America and urging that nation to get into
the war to help Britain. Both these Pankhursts were becoming the darlings of the Government.

Both were riding a high crest of popularity, so welcome
to them after the past years of grim struggle. Wealthy
industrialists contributed money to the W.S.P.U., and
politicians courted them. Instead of being scorned as un-

natural females, they were hailed as champions of law
and respectability and all the old-fashioned virtues.

But both Adela and Sylvia were shocked. Adela had
found her horticultural studies futile. To keep her promise to her mother not to engage in agitation in Britain,
Adela had migrated to Australia, where she immediately
hit the newspaper headlines with her activities in behalf
of the ill-paid seamen.

Sylvia was now known as "Red" Sylvia. She scorned
the war as a battle between capitalist powers to redivide
the world for their own advantages; she said the poor
would inevitably suffer from such a war, and was out-
spokenly against it. Her newspaper was now the *Workers'
Dreadnought,* and this Pankhurst was still looked upon
as a subversive by the British Government.

Emmeline paid one call upon Sylvia, who had become
a source of embarrassment to the mother in the mother's
role of defender of the Empire. Sylvia, said Emmeline,
had her choice. "You can come with me or stay here with
these women." It was a final ultimatum.

Sylvia stayed with her East End women and her principles. Mother and daughter never spoke to each other
again. In 1916, when Mrs. Pankhurst was in America
urging that country to get into the war, she heard Sylvia
had organized a rally in London against conscripting
troops into the army. She cabled the W.S.P.U.: "Strongly
repudiate Sylvia's foolish and unpatriotic conduct. Re-
gret I cannot prevent use of name." And she had this
published in the newspapers.

It is not to be supposed that the break was easy for

either one. Sylvia had long adored her mother, and Emmeline could not forget her memories of Sylvia comforting her at Harry's deathbed. But both were of a breed to put their causes above their emotions.

By 1917 the status of women in Britain had changed. They were entrenched in jobs and offices. They were emancipated. The Government bowed to the inevitable. Cabinet members asked Emmeline and other suffrage leaders if an act giving votes to a limited number of women (with property qualifications) would be acceptable.

The suffragettes enthusiastically approved, and the act was finally passed just before December, 1918. At long last a woman could vote and hold major political office in Britain! Emmeline heard some people say the militant suffrage fight had never been necessary, and that the war would inevitably have brought women their rights.

She knew this was nonsense. Wars had come and gone, and never before had they brought the vote. France and other countries were in this same war, yet their women still had their long struggle for suffrage ahead of them.

When the act went into effect, Christabel immediately announced her candidacy for Parliament in the constituency of Smethwick. Emmeline and Flora Drummond threw themselves vigorously into the campaign, yet Christabel lost. Smethwick was a working-class area, and Christabel did not know how to talk to working people.

The blow was a bitter one to Emmeline. The honour of being the first woman to be seated as a member of Parliament went to the American-born Nancy, Viscountess Astor, in 1919. Had Lady Astor ever worked for that honour? Had she ever been in gaol? Never.

In a sense, both Emmeline and Christabel then retired from politics. Full suffrage for all the women of Britain was inevitable, and the campaign for the vote was finished. Both declared that it was fine for a woman to be able to cast her ballot, but the life of a politician was no fit place for a lady.

The Pankhursts, however, were not finished. There were causes in plenty for them, and Emmeline and her daughters stayed in the public limelight.

Sometimes they were celebrities, sometimes nuisances; they were famous or notorious, depending upon one's viewpoint. At times they were called sinners, at others they were referred to as saints but always they moved across the national and international sky like shooting stars, making the world more colourful for their flights.

In 1919 the Russian revolution came, and Emmeline and Sylvia battled it out publicly. Mrs. Pankhurst went on successful speaking tours since she was considered an authority on the subject, having been sent, semi-officially, to Russia to try to boost morale there during the war. "Red" Sylvia was equally outspoken and got six months in gaol as an enemy agent.

When Emmeline found interest in that dying down, she quickly picked up another cause. She lectured on the forbidden, unmentioned topic of venereal disease. She drew people to her lectures. It did not seem improper to go to hear such a queenly, old-fashioned mother figure. Though times had changed with the advent of auto-

mobiles, electricity and telephones, Emmeline clung to
her long velvet gowns and kept her long white hair piled
on top of her head under a lace mantilla.

In 1926 Emmeline returned to England and decided
that men were making such a mess of politics she would
have to change her mind. Early in 1927 she announced
she would be standing as a candidate for Parliament in
the next general election.

The news was a sensation. For one reason, Emmeline
was now sixty-nine years old. For another, the fire-eating
suffrage radical promised to campaign on the most conservative of platforms. And for another, she intended to
invade Sylvia's own bailiwick, the East End, as her constituency for election.

All London was agog at the thought of the two Pankhursts in a political duel, and looked forward to fire-
works.

But Emmeline had overestimated her physical strength,
which was undermined by all her sufferings in prison.
By Christmas of 1927 she was having long spells of ill-
ness. She was unable to do any campaigning. But in
March, 1928, she did rouse herself to appear in the gallery of the House of Commons at the final reading of
the Equal Suffrage Bill, which gave full suffrage to all
women of twenty-one years of age.

It seemed symbolic, as if her work was finally over.
Shortly after that she took to her bed, and her condition
became alarming. Christabel was always with her. Adela,
in Australia, was too far away to come, but Sylvia wrote
and begged her mother to see her. Strict with herself
as always, Emmeline refused.

Mrs. Pankhurst died on June 14, 1928. In one month she would have been seventy years old.

Most of those years had been given to public service to a great ideal. At her death, newspapers all over the world printed columns of her life story; statesmen acclaimed her; clergymen gave sermons on her greatness. The *Daily Mail* of London wrote:

"Mrs. Pankhurst had . . . a superb courage, and with it that white-hot enthusiasm which gave to the campaign, with all its hysterical excesses, a kind of wild dignity. . . . She and her followers had turned women's suffrage, until then a subject for academic or facetious discussion, into a question for which men as well as women were ready to fight to the last ditch."

Nearly all her old friends came to the funeral, among them Annie Kenney, Mrs. Drummond, Mr. and Mrs. Pethick-Lawrence and Mrs. Despard. Sylvia and Christabel were there, but though the sisters sat near each other they were united only by their love for their mother. They were enemies in everything else.

It is strange but, of all Emmeline's daughters, Sylvia was the one who grew to be most like her in fighting determination and flamboyant style—not Christabel.

Christabel had grown remote from worldly matters. She became convinced that people were impure—especially men—and could only be changed by spiritual regeneration. For a while she shocked people by lecturing on the need for sexual chastity; then she became a Second Adventist preacher.

She lived a pleasant life, always welcomed as a house

guest in the homes of wealthy friends, and died in Southern California on February 13, 1958, at seventy-eight.

Adela's career was both turbulent and strange. When she first went to Australia, she had flamed into immediate prominence as a champion of trade unions. She married Tom Walsh, an organizer of the seamen's union, and their joint efforts helped secure better wages and living standards for Australian seamen. But once that was done, they tried to put on the brakes.

They split with the more militant trade unions. They became conservative. Adela turned her interests to Japan, and admired its new, rising power, not understanding fully its militaristic, fascistic character. After Pearl Harbour she was interned in Australia for enemy activity. After she was released, she gave up public life and devoted herself to her four children.

She died in May of 1961, converted to Roman Catholicism, forgiven in Australia for her brief flirtation with fascism and remembered gratefully for her work in benefiting the lot of seamen.

Of all the sisters, Sylvia's rise to prominence was the highest and lasted the longest. At first her career seemed erratic. She became a communist but quarrelled with Lenin, who publicly spanked Comrade Sylvia Pankhurst with an essay entitled *Left Wing Communism: An Infantile Sickness,* directed at her for being impractical and romantic.

She then broke off her communist affiliations, but, unlike Adela, she did not change her fundamental ideas. She went on publishing her newspaper and championing the underdog.

She fell in love with Silvio Corio, an Italian exiled from his country for his progressive beliefs. They did not marry because Sylvia thought the marriage ceremony an instrument of subjection to both men and women, but— contrary to all the scandalized prophecies—she and Corio were happily devoted to each other. Their son, Richard Keir Pethick Pankhurst, never suffered from his illegitimacy, but grew up intelligent and well adjusted.

She threw all her splendid Pankhurst fire and enthusiasm and her writing talents into the fight against fascism at a time when this was not popular. People were still either laughing at the "little man with his moustache" or saying Hitler and Mussolini were just the kind of strong men their countries needed when Sylvia began her long, persistent fight against them.

At first her articles and speeches were considered a nuisance, the work of a crackpot. But when Italy invaded Ethiopia in 1935 and Sylvia became Ethiopia's champion, people began to listen to her. She made them ashamed. Britain, as one of the leaders in the League of Nations, could have stopped this. They could have applied sanctions to Italy, depriving that country of the oil it needed, and stopped the invasion.

It might have even stopped a second World War. If the Fascists had been taught such a lesson right in the beginning, they might have thought twice about another aggression.

This was Sylvia's message to the world when the Germans next tried out their air force in Spain. Once again Sylvia was speaking in Trafalgar Square and in the

Albert Hall, as in the suffrage days, and calling for a Popular Front against the dictators.

She and Corio published the *New Times and Ethiopia News* for twenty years. It was an excellent paper, dealing with the whole fight against fascism everywhere. Prominent writers, educators, politicians and political refugees from Germany, Spain and Italy and Africa contributed to it, and it was widely read. It was a tremendous force in the world struggle that was shaping up.

In those years it is not likely that she had much, if any, communication with Adela, since Sylvia could not tolerate her younger sister's admiration for the policies of Japan. But Christabel did pay her one visit. She came to insist that Sylvia marry Corio and legitimize her son.

But Sylvia was at last free of any domination by Christabel, and she could hardly keep from laughing. Who was this spinster—so proud of her pretty looks, yet so shocked by men and sex—to be telling her of her responsibilities as a mother? She told Christabel to mind her own business, and never saw her again

Indeed, Sylvia, never a pretty girl, was having a late blooming. Happy in her personal life and justified in all her long political struggle as Britain finally had to go to war against fascism, she had become a vibrant and attractive woman. All through World War II she was recognized as a prophet and a fighter. She appeared on television and made broadcasts, and the big newspapers sought her out to write special articles for them.

When the war was over, she went on fighting. She quickly spotted the fact that the peace terms would let Italy retain some Ethiopian territory, and she and her son and Corio forced this secret arrangement out into the open and attacked it furiously. The treaty makers backed down. Once again Sylvia had helped in a victory for the underdog.

Corio died in 1954, so Sylvia and Richard went, in the spring of 1956, to live in Ethiopia. There she was treated as an empress, second only to Emperor Haile Selassie. She had a home and could at last rest on her laurels, but, being a Pankhurst, she did not. For the next six years of her life she had frequent conferences with African leaders, giving what help she could as they threw off the shackles of colonial domination; founded a social service centre in Addis Ababa; published *Ethiopia: a Cultural History;* built a hospital; promoted the holding of an International Women's Seminar in Ethiopia; and printed a newspaper.

She died at seventy-eight years of age, on September 27, 1960, and her funeral was attended by the Emperor and by diplomatic representatives of all the nations stationed in Ethiopia. The funeral oration was given by the Minister of the Interior, who said:

"Sylvia Pankhurst, the Emperor and the Ethiopian people, whom you sincerely and honestly served, now stand weeping around you. Your history will live forever. . . . May God, who has surely witnessed your noble deeds, keep you in a place of honour."

Emmeline Pankhurst's portrait was hung in the National Portrait Gallery, and a statue of her stands in Victoria Tower Gardens. In 1936 Christabel had been created a Dame Commander of the British Empire (D.B.E.) for her suffrage work, and in 1937 Adela was awarded the George VI Coronation Medal for the same cause. "Red" Sylvia was omitted from any British honours list, but memorials to her abound in Ethiopia.

The true memorial to the amazing Pankhurst family lies in the hearts of all women everywhere. Those women already emancipated can thank them for the schools they can attend, the professions they can choose, the husbands they can love as equal partners, the citizenship they have. Those still struggling for equality can look to the example set by Emmeline and her daughters.

In fact, even in the most advanced democracies, women have not yet won complete equality, and Emmeline Pankhurst's restless ghost is still whispering: "Courage, my splendid ones—scratch their eyes out!"

BIBLIOGRAPHY

Kamm, Josephine. *The Story of Mrs. Pankhurst.* London: Methuen and Co., Ltd., 1961.

Mitchell, David. *The Fighting Pankhursts.* London: Jonathan Cape, 1967.

Morgan, Kenneth O. *Keir Hardie.* London: Oxford University Press, 1967.

Pankhurst, Dame Christabel. *Unshackled: The Story of How We Won the Vote.* London: Hutchinsons and Co., 1959.

Pankhurst, Emmeline. *My Own Story.* London: Eveleigh Nash, 1914.

Pankhurst, E. Sylvia. *The Life of Emmeline Pankhurst.* London: T. Werner Laurie, Ltd., 1935.

———. *The Suffragette Movement.* London and New York: Longmans, Green and Company, 1931.

Peck, Mary Gray. *Carrie Chapman Catt.* New York: H. W. Wilson Company, 1944.

Pethick-Lawrence, Emmeline. *My Part in a Changing World.* London: Gollancz, 1938.

Walsh, Adela Pankhurst, and Walsh, Thomas. *Japan As Viewed by Foreigners.* Sydney, Australia: Robert Dey Son & Co., 1940.

185

————. *Suffrage Speeches from the Dock, Made at Conspiracy Trial, Old Bailey, 1912*. London: The Women's Press, 1912.

————. *The Trial of the Suffragette Leaders, Court Proceedings*. London: The Women's Press, 1908.

INDEX

187

ABOUT THE AUTHOR

Writing and traveling fascinate Iris Noble. "In what other profession," she says, "could I carry my office with me? Typewriter in hand, suitcase stuffed with reams of paper, I can be off to work and yet at the same time visit all the exciting places in the world."

She was born in Calgary, Canada of American parents, and during her early years lived on a ranch in the Crow's Nest Pass. When she was eleven, she moved with her family to Oregon, where she attended elementary school in Portland and graduated from Oregon City High School. She majored in English at the University of Oregon and did graduate work at Stanford University in California. She worked as a secretary and as a publicity-advertising director before her marriage to author Hollister Noble in 1941. When they moved soon afterward to New York City, Mrs. Noble began writing magazine articles and gradually moved into books. She has been writing exclusively for young people—biography and fiction—ever since.

For a time she made her home in California, but the urge to travel has sent her throughout Europe, Asia, Africa and the Middle East, researching for new biographical subjects.